Living Life GOD'S WAY

by

JOHN GALANTI

WORD & SPIRIT
PUBLISHING

Living Life God's Way

ISBN: 978-1-949106-41-1

Published by Word and Spirit Publishing
P.O. Box 701403
Tulsa, Oklahoma 74170
wordandspiritpublishing.com

Dedication

I first want to thank my wife, Tina. I love you, honey, you are always so supportive of me. Also, I want to thank my grandmother for laying a foundation during a time that no one else thought to. I want to thank my mother for always showing me love. I want to thank my mother-in-law, Susan Sansone, without whose guidance this book could not have happened. Finally, I want to thank Christ Fellowship for helping me be part of a community and finding the narrow path.

Preface

MORE than a year ago, I began writing a "Verse of the Day" on my *Average John* Facebook page. Looking back, I can see that I had been focusing on the wrong things—the 24-hour news cycle, talk radio, and other negative distractions. The political divide in our country consumed me, along with many other worldly distractions that Jesus warned us about.

I was missing what was important: God, Jesus, the Holy Spirit, and the Scriptures. Although I started my day in prayer, giving myself a good foundation for the day, I would go directly from that positive influence to watching television news or listening to talk radio news. I would get all worked up, filling myself with all the negativity that surrounds us every day. So, on September 7, 2019, I deleted the news sources from my social media and eliminated 90 percent of the news I was watching and listening to, replacing it with godly content such as "Podcast from Chip Ingram," Dr. David Jeremiah of "Turning Point," worship music, books, and many other positive and godly sources. Since making these changes I feel like a different person, a God-filled person. Although I still have so much to learn, I now believe I am heading in the right direction.

Don't get me wrong. I still believe those afraid of losing their power, influence, and money are purposefully dividing us, mostly through fear and hate. However, the good news is that widespread corruption is finally being exposed. I pay enough attention to stay informed, but I now pray for our leaders on both sides of the aisle and our President much more often.

As I wrote this book, I tried to take a common sense approach to the Bible verses, including my own thoughts about each verse. By no means do I claim to have a firm grasp on Scripture, just the opposite. I am a student trying to learn each day, understanding that I have a long way to go, as do most of us. I found that sharing the Verse of the Day on my *Average John* Facebook page, helped *me* more than anyone else, but I was hoping to help a few others along the way.

I share my spiritual journey with the love of my life, Tina Marie Angelina Sansone Galanti (she will love the use of her full name). Without her, this journey would be much harder and not nearly as much fun! We attend an extraordinary church here in Jupiter, Florida—Christ Fellowship. I now understand how important it is to surround myself with other Christ-minded friends and followers. I also see the importance of being part of a Bible-teaching church that reaches out to help so many others. We have met some amazing people that have helped us become part of a community that is seeking the same goals.

I think that one of the biggest gifts I have received since beginning my journey is in learning to be content. Finding our way to God does not mean everything becomes easy. If anything, it is just the opposite. God *tells* us there will be suffering and hard times. What I now appreciate is knowing God is always with me, helping me get through those tough times.

My Story

IN church, our pastor points out that telling our story of how we came to Christ and how it came about that Jesus opened the door for us to have a personal relationship with God, might help others find their way. Although I am not one who particularly likes telling my own story, here is my testimony.

As I was growing up, my parents seldom spoke of religion. I was only about a year old when my mom and dad got divorced. My mother then married my stepfather, Tom, who was an atheist, so there just was no talk of God from him. Fortunately, he did not stop my mother from celebrating holidays like Christmas and Easter. I didn't meet my father until I was around eleven. I don't blame any of my hard times on not knowing my dad during my early childhood, that's just the way it was.

We had a non-traditional upbringing to say the least. My mom was raised Catholic, but other than celebrating the traditional holidays, she did not practice it at all. She did try to follow some of the church traditions like having us get our Holy Communion, but most likely my grandmother orchestrated that. My mom and Tom smoked pot in the house every night. They would at least shut their bedroom door, but I always wondered about the smell that came from their room until I was old enough to figure out what it was.

I have one brother, Joe, one sister, Annette, and three stepbrothers, Kenny, Keith, and Gary. As the youngest of the family, I understood as a preteen that my entire family smoked pot and did harder drugs. My sister also dated a guy, Al, who pretty much lived with us and also did drugs, sold drugs, and drank a great deal. My parents hardly supervised us. I was around eleven when I first started smoking pot. Then drinking followed shortly thereafter, along with dating. My brothers had big parties that I went to, all the while thinking this was normal.

My entire teenage years consisted of partying. I smoked pot every day, all day, starting before school. At night I drank, went to keg parties, smoked and did other drugs, and hung out with girls, all of which was completely unsupervised and unrestricted. As time went on, the drugs got harder, the drinking got out of control, and my life was a mess—like, rock bottom mess.

That is just some of my background, and I'll spare you the remainder of the details, but this was the point where I knew I needed God and help. It was odd. Sometimes during parties in my first apartment, I would lay on the couch and read the Bible. My roommate and his girlfriend would laugh and ask why I was reading it. I normally didn't say much about it, and honestly, I didn't understand most of what I was reading.

One night after doing some very heavy drugs, I had just had enough. I left the apartment and started walking through a snowstorm until I found myself standing in front of my grandmother's little church, which was only about a mile from my home. Something made me go in (I now know what), and I just sat in the back row and prayed. I remember telling God I needed Him, and vaguely remember accepting Jesus and asking for His help.

It was soon after that night that my life began to change. At the time I didn't realize that changes were happening because I had asked Jesus to come into my life, but looking back now I understand the blessing I received. Days later, I went down to the recruiter's office and joined the military—something I would have never done in the past. I had been kicked out of school with a semester remaining until graduation—my life was a mess—but the recruiters were great. They put me in a delayed entry program and set me up to get my diploma at night school. They let me know that once I completed my schooling, I would be off to boot camp.

The next day, I approached a picnic bench where some of my friends were hanging out. I was wearing a black leather biker's jacket, the kind with many zippered pockets. Knowing I needed a change, I started emptying my pockets, giving them all the drugs that I had. I told them I was done, quitting drugs, and joining the service. They laughed and tried to pass me their communal joint, but I walked away and never did drugs again. I am sad to say that a high percentage of the guys I grew up with have either died or are messed up from drugs. However, I am happy that a few have found God and are living much better lives.

Over the next 30 years, my life was much better. After getting out of the military, I got married and had two children, Deanna and Michael, who changed my ability to love another human being. However, I never lost my drinking problem, nor did I surrender myself to God or even bother to learn the teachings of Jesus. I always knew God was with me, but I took what he did for me for granted. Throughout those thirty years, I had some very tough times, but also some amazing times. I see now that the tough times were mostly because I was still an alcoholic, never content, and I had never fully committed myself to God.

Now in my fifties, I am married to the love of my life, Tina, who is truly a godsend. Life was pretty good as I entered this decade. I was still an alcoholic, but at least a controlled one, I liked to think. Looking back, I was anything but. Tina and I knew something was missing in our lives. We often spoke about joining a church where we felt connected, but finding one was a hard task. I never wanted to invest the time or enough effort into what I now see to be the most important investment one can make.

One day while traveling for work, I called Tina and she was very excited. She told me that she had found the church we needed to join. While going through the channels, she had landed on a sermon from Pastor Todd Mullins. She knew immediately this was the church we should start watching and possibly join. At the end of the service, she discovered that this church was right in the town where we live, and we would be able to attend instead of just watching it on TV.

Since joining Christ Fellowship, I've finally surrendered my life to God, and made Jesus my Lord and Savior. God has answered so many of my prayers. I still drink, but only on social occasions, and normally don't have more than two beers or a glass of wine. My wife and I were both baptized in the ocean on April 29, 2018, and I now truly understand the meaning of being Born Again, along with the feeling of the Holy Spirit entering my life. God has opened my mind to understand the Scriptures; He has fixed things in my family life that I prayed for, He has helped me eliminate my alcoholism and has shown me what it is to be content.

I could go on—God is in my life every day. I start my day in prayer, giving the first of me always, but I don't stop there. I make sure to exercise my spiritual life more than my physical life, work life, or personal life. I also now understand the importance of trusting God with our finances. This was a big step for me, and I am so happy we made that decision. God is the biggest part of my life, not just a box to check that makes me feel like I completed a task.

BELOW is a list of some of the sources and publications that have helped me stay focused on God every day. I hope some of them can help you get started or continue your journey. I recommend starting a daily routine that keeps God first in your life.

- Chip Ingram App
- Turning Point
- www.gochristfelloship.com
- Moody Radio
- Hillsong Worship music
- Joel Osteen, *Today's Word*
- Watch more faith base movies, such as *The Chosen*. Download the app.
- The Bible App.
- And of course, the most important, the Bible!

NOW I want to share with you some of the "Verses of the Day" I have posted on my Facebook page, starting with one of my favorite verses. You will notice that I didn't include my thoughts after some verses, this is because some verses need no additional comment. At the end of several chapters, I have added a group of 10 verses that address important issues in our lives. These include verses on prayer, thankfulness, forgiveness, deceit, faith, and love.

I want to point out how I picked the verses each day. I point this out because I believe this exercise was extremely important in helping me create a daily routine. Each day I would start with prayer, speaking directly with God and forming my relationship with Him. Afterwards I would ask for His guidance as I opened my Bible in picking a verse that would speak to me. Some days a verse would come right to me, while others would take some time. I strongly suggest getting in a similar routine, even doing the same that I have done and adding your own thoughts. I believe doing this activity helped open my eyes in a way that was not present prior to my commitment to the Word.

GOD bless us all!

Verse of the Day

PHILIPPIANS 4:13

For I can do all things through Christ, who gives me strength.

THIS is one of my favorite verses. It really helped when I was just beginning my spiritual journey, and still does today. This verse has gotten me through tough times, times of doubt, times of temptation, and times of sorrow.

Another thing I love about what Paul is telling the Philippians is found in the verses before this one. Verses 4:11-12 show why 4:13 is so powerful, and how it will lead you to a life of contentment instead of worry:

Not that I was ever in need, for I have learned how to be content with whatever I have. I know how to live on almost nothing or with everything. I have learned the secret of living in every situation, whether it is with a full stomach or empty, with plenty or little (vv. 12-13).

The secret is verse 4:13. *For I can do all things through Christ, who gives me strength.*

It is easy to be content when things are good, but where do we get our strength during those challenging times? Are you equipped to stay content when things get rough? Because they will—that's just life!

From this point, I will be sharing the verses that have helped me every day since I started surrendering myself to God and the Lord Jesus.The time I spent each day doing my *Verse of the Day* helped me more than I can explain. I did miss some days, but I strove to stay consistent in my practice and dedication to spending time in the Scriptures. I hope it will help you, too.

Everything we need to have a successful life is in the Bible.

CHAPTER 1

January

TODAY in church, our pastor shared a quote that is so true. If more people would think this way, we would live in a much better world. In a time when our country is being divided for mostly selfish reasons, this is the message that needs to be heard:

"What unites us is greater than what divides us."

No matter whether we are rich or poor, what our ethnicity is, what gender we are, or what political party we support, we know that we have Jesus to unite us and bring us to knowing our Father. We are all children of the same God! Thank you, Pastor Todd!

January 1

Happy New Year! Time for a clear vision for this New Year. Today is the perfect opportunity to start a new life in Christ and leave the old life behind.

You can pray to the Lord Jesus yourself, in your own words. Or, if you prefer, I offer my own prayer as guidance:

Lord Jesus, I ask You to forgive my sins and save me from eternal separation from God. By faith, I accept Your work and death on the cross as sufficient payment for my sins. Thank You for providing the way for me to know You and have a relationship with my heavenly Father. Through faith in You, I have eternal life. Thank You also for hearing my prayers and loving me unconditionally. Please give me the strength, wisdom, and determination to walk in the center of Your will. In Jesus' name, amen.

If you have just prayed this prayer for the first time, congratulations!

You have received Christ as your Savior and have made the best decision you will ever make—one that will change your life forever! Now put in the work to learn all that Jesus was teaching us. It does help to find a Bible-teaching church that you trust to guide you.

Verse of the Day

PROVERBS 2:20-22 TPT

Follow those who follow wisdom and stay on the right path. For all my godly lovers will enjoy life to the fullest and will inherit their destinies. But the treacherous ones who love darkness will not only lose all they could have had—they will lose even their souls!

I cannot understand why people do not accept what God offers us. It seems that people are passionate about their commitment to earthly pursuits, but lack the same passion in living God's Word. Then they wonder why their lives are not in order!

January 2

Verse of the Day

1 PETER 2:1 NLT

So get rid of all evil behavior. Be done with all deceit, hypocrisy, jealousy, and all unkind speech.

It is easy to continue to live in the dark, but I know how painful that is. Look toward the light. It takes effort but is worth every minute invested.

January 4

Verse of the Day

EPHESIANS 3:17 NLT

Then Christ will make his home in your hearts as you trust in him. Your roots will grow down into God's love and keep you strong.

I am so thankful that I chose the path to seek God and all that He offers us. I know what it is like to be on the other path, to be tormented and feel lost. I will never go back to that life. Thank you God!

January 5

Verse of the Day

PROVERBS 3:13-15

Blessed are those who find wisdom, those who gain understanding, for she is more profitable than silver and yields better returns than gold. She is more precious than rubies; nothing you desire can compare with her.

Wisdom is found in the Word! God gave us the ability to gain His wisdom through His Word, as well as instructions on how to use it. Now it is up to us to take the right steps. What a comfort!

January 7

Verse of the Day

LUKE 18:17

Truly I tell you, anyone who will not receive the kingdom of God like a little child will never enter it.

When we were children, we listened to what our parents taught us. God, our Father, is asking for that kind of love, trust, and obedience.

January 9

Verse of the Day

1 TIMOTHY 4:1

The Spirit clearly says that in later times some will abandon the faith and follow deceiving spirits and things taught by demons.

I believe there is a constant battle for our souls, we will be tempted constantly, and only the full armor of God can protect us as I repeatedly have said. Be mindful of what you follow!

January 10

Verse of the Day

1 CORINTHIANS 13:13

And now these three things remain: faith, hope, and love. But the greatest of these is love.

If we let hate guide any area of our life, we are letting God down and inviting evil in. Choose love!

January 11

Verse of the Day

PROVERBS 28:20

A faithful person will be richly blessed, but one eager to get rich will not go unpunished.

It's not money that is evil, it is the *love* of money that displeases God. We can also be richly blessed with other things besides money. I understand this now more than ever. If we have been blessed, we need take the time to pass our blessings on to others in need. Benevolence pleases God tremendously.

January 12

Verse of the Day

JOHN 14:15-17

If you love me, keep my commands. And I will ask the Father, and he will give you another advocate to help you and be with you forever—the Spirit is truth. The world cannot accept him, because it neither sees him nor knows him. But you know him, for he lives with you and will be in you.

You cannot understand the feeling of the Holy Spirit that Jesus was offering until you make the commitment that Jesus requires. However, once you do this it will become clear. Ask and you will receive! Knock and the door will be opened! Put more in your spiritual training than you do your earthly training, and the spiritual rewards will far outweigh any earthly rewards.

January 13

Verse of the Day

JEREMIAH 15:21

I will save you from the hands of the wicked and deliver you from the grasp of the cruel.

I don't know how much more reassurance we need to make a commitment to God and Jesus. We have heard of the spiritual realm, where good battles evil for our souls. Is this something to brush aside or is it worth looking into?

January 14

Verse of the Day

MATTHEW 4:3-4

The tempter came to him and said, "If you are the Son of God, tell these stones to become bread." Jesus answered, "It is written: Man shall not live by bread alone, but on every word that comes from the mouth of God."

We will all be tempted in this world by material things, but if we keep the bigger picture in mind, the greater route down the narrow road will be easier for us to follow.

January 15

Verse of the Day

PSALM 7:1-2

Lord my God, I take refuge in you; save and deliver me from all who pursue me, or they will tear me apart like a lion and rip me to pieces with no one to rescue me.

This may sound harsh, but if sin consumes us, it will feel like our life is being torn apart. God offers us this refuge in Him; again, all we have to do is accept Him.

January 16

Verse of the Day

MATTHEW 12:30-31

"Whoever is not with me is against me, and whoever does not gather with me scatters. And I tell you, every kind of sin and slander can be forgiven, but blasphemy against the Spirit will not be forgiven."

If you don't think this is important than you are a much bigger risk taker than I. It is one thing not to believe, or to be uninformed. However, to speak against God is just unimaginable to me.

January 20

Verse of the Day

JOHN 3:19-20

"This is the verdict: Light has come into the world, but people loved the darkness instead of the light because their deeds were evil. Everyone who does evil hates the light, and will not come into the light for fear that their deeds will be exposed."

If we are on the wrong path now, or were in the past, we understand this verse better than most. I know because I was on that path. The good news is we have the ability and means to change it if we so choose.

January 24

Verse of the Day

LUKE 10:23-24

Then he turned to his disciples and said privately, "Blessed are the eyes that see what you see. For I tell you that many prophets and kings wanted to see but did not see it, and to hear what you hear but did not hear it."

Do people understand how significant it was to be alive when Jesus walked the Earth? It took me a long time to grasp that God came to Earth, gave us the instruction manual, and loves us so much that He offered us the opportunity to be saved.

January 26

Verse of the Day

1 JOHN 2:17

The world and its desires pass away, but whoever does the will of God lives forever.

It is easy to get ourselves caught up in worldly things. The problem is that "things" do not last, but our afterlife is eternal. If we understand fully what He is offering, how can anyone turn away from it?

Take Time to Reflect

IF you've ever said to yourself, "I don't even have time to think," then you know how hard it is to concentrate when you're being bombarded with noise from all sides. It can be even harder to hold on to peace when we don't make time to read His Word. God does not often shout to get our attention. Instead, the Bible says that He speaks in *"a still, small voice."* What can we do to put ourselves in a position to hear God's voice? The key is to make time every day away from the busyness and distractions. If we find a room in our house, outside under the trees, or in some other place where we can be still for a few minutes each day to spend time with Him, He will renew our spirit and restore our peace.

January 27

Verse of the Day

REVELATION 18:1-2

After all this I saw another angel coming down from heaven. He had great authority, and the earth was illuminated by his splendor. With a mighty voice he shouted: Fallen! Fallen is Babylon the Great! She has become a dwelling for demons and a haunt for every impure spirit a haunt for every unclean bird, a haunt for every unclean and detestable animal.

Put on the whole armor of God! Pray always. We do not want to go through difficult times alone without God's protection from the powers of evil. We may think we have this world figured out on our own, but what happens when things get really tough?

January 28

Verse of the Day

MARK 5:34

He said to her, "Daughter, your faith has healed you. Go in peace and be freed from your suffering."

This verse says to me two big things. First, it tells us Jesus was God on Earth. Next, it shows the power of faith. I would suggest reading this entire story to get the full impact.

January 29

Verse of the Day

MATTHEW 16:26-27

"What good will it be for someone to gain the whole world, yet forfeit their soul? For the Son of Man is going to come in his Father's glory with angles, and then he will reward each person according to what they have done."

What price are we willing to pay for earthly rewards? Jesus offers us everything, and still many turn away, towards this world's temptations. I repeated this verse because it can not be said enough.

January 30

Verse of the Day

PSALM 53:4-5

Do all these evildoers know nothing? They devour my people as though eating bread; they never call on God. But there they are, overwhelmed with dread, where there was nothing to dread. God scattered the bones of those who attack you; you put them to shame, for God despised them.

So many people live in turmoil when they don't have to. They live in "dread" because they never call on God. We can choose to live overwhelmed, or reach out to God and begin a relationship that will change our lives. I know this through personal experience.

January 31

Verse of the Day

PROVERBS 11:23

The desire of the righteous ends only in good, but the hope for the wicked only in wrath.

God must think, "I have laid out so many warnings. What is it going to take to get their attention?"

CHAPTER 2

February

JUST because you don't understand everything about God, the prophets, and Jesus is no reason to reject them. Non-believers along with many believers disregard the facts or don't bother to research what the facts of scriptures are, and unfortunately they often form a predetermined opinion. What saddens me about this is, because of their actions, or lack of action they will be missing out on the greatest offer EVER!

February 1 ____________________________

Verse of the Day

PSALM 23

The Lord is my shepherd, I lack nothing. He makes me lie down in green pastures, he leads me beside quiet waters, he refreshes my soul. He guides me along the right paths for his name sake. Even though I walk through the darkest valley. I will fear no evil, for you are with me; your rod and your staff, they comfort me. You prepare a table before me in the presence of my enemies. You anoint my head with oil; my cup overflows. Surely your goodness and love will follow me all the days of my life, and I will dwell in the house of the Lord forever.

In loving memory of my Grandma! She tried to tell me so many times, it just took me many years to realize it. Thank you!

February 3___________________________

Verse of the Day

MATTHEW 24:12-13

Because of the increase of wickedness, the love will grow cold, but the one who stands firm to the end will be saved.

Are we equipped to stand firm? Do we wear the full armor of God to protect us from evil? Are we confident that at the end of our lives we will be where we want to be?

February 4___________________________

Verse of the Day

JOHN 10:10

"The thief comes only to steal and kill and destroy; I have come that they may have life, and have it to the full."

We need to guard ourselves and pick the right paths. Temptation comes in small things first, but will eventually consume us if left unchecked. The good news is that Jesus offered us another way.

February 9

Verse of the Day

PSALM 97:10-11

Let those who love the Lord hate evil. For he guards the lives of his faithful ones and delivers them from the hand of the wicked. Light shines on the righteous and joy on the upright in heart.

It is hard to explain how it feels to hand your life over to the Lord. If I had to use one word to explain, it would be "contentment." I felt like a massive weight was lifted off my shoulders. I am proud to say that I am now one of the faithful, but I still need daily reminders to stay on the right path. These include prayer, reading Scripture, and many other daily spiritual exercises.

February 11

Verse of the Day

ROMANS 2:1

You, therefore, have no excuse, you who pass judgement on someone else, for at whatever point you judge another, you are condemning yourself, because you who pass judgement do the same things.

We see and hear so much judgement today. If we know the Bible, we will know our sins! Are any of us so perfect that we can judge others? We need to look at ourselves and make sure things are right within us before being passing judgement on others. We will all be judged when that time comes, but will we all be prepared?

February 12 ___

Verse of the Day

LUKE 21:34-36

"Be careful, or your hearts will be weighed down with carousing, drunkenness, and the anxieties of life, and that day will close on you suddenly like a trap. For it will come on all those who live on the face of the whole earth. Be always on watch, and pray that you may be able to escape all that is about to happen, and that you may be able to stand before the Son of Man."

We will all stand in judgement one day, but Jesus prepares us for that day. He left us with all the proof; He fulfilled the words of the prophets, healed the sick, raised the dead, performed many miracles, and was resurrected three days after His death. His birth, death, and resurrection were predicted in Scripture. Nevertheless, so many still question who He was in addition to the words He spoke. That day will come quickly, without warning just as promised. Be ready for it!

February 13 ______________________________

Verse of the Day

MATTHEW 6:9-13

"This, then, is how you should pray: Our Father in heaven, hallowed be your name, your kingdom come, your will be done, on earth as it is in heaven. Give us today our daily bread. And forgive us our debts, as we also have forgiven our debtors. And lead us not to temptation, but deliver us from the evil one."

Prayer should be simple. To me it is more about having a relationship with God in which we speak to Him plainly and directly. He already knows what we need; He just wants to hear it from us.

February 14 ______________________________

Verse of the Day

MATTHEW 7:1-2

"Do not judge, or you too will be judged. For in the same way you judge others, you will be judged, and with the measure you use, it will be measured to you."

If we disagree with someone and pray for them, then both parties benefit. The business world calls that a win-win. In addition, we will be pleasing God, instead of disappointing Him. I guess that is a win-win-win!

February 17 ____________________

Verse of the Day

ROMANS 6:23

For the wages of sin is death, but the gift of God is eternal life in Christ Jesus our Lord.

We all know when we are sinning. Our merciful God offers us a way out provided we accept His offer. My comments may be repetitious, but these teachings have been around for thousands of years, repeating themselves, and still so many choose to ignore them. (Another reason for repetition is that the various authors of the Bible were all preaching the same message.) I hope you choose to listen, learn, and live them!

February 19 ____________________

Verse of the Day

1 PETER 1:8-9

Though you have not seen him, you love him; and even though you do not see him now, you believe in him and are filled with inexpressible and glorious joy, for you are receiving the end result of your faith, the salvation of your souls.

I don't know anything better to receive!

February 20 ________________________________

Verse of the Day

PSALM 52:2-5

You who practice deceit, your tongue plots destruction; it is like a sharpened razor. You love evil rather than good, falsehood rather than speaking the truth. You love every harmful word you deceitful tongue! Surely God will bring you down to everlasting ruin: He will snatch you up and pluck you from your tent; he will uproot you from the land of the living.

Our actions and words have consequences, so we need to choose wisely what we say. Seek truth, and the truth will set us free!

February 21

Verse of the Day

1 PETER 1:24-25

All people are like grass, and all their glory is like the flower of a field; the grass withers and the flowers fall, but the word of the Lord endures forever.

February 23 ____________________

Verse of the Day

JOHN 12:35

Then Jesus told them, "You are going to have the light just a little while longer. Walk while you have the light, before darkness overtakes you. Whoever walks in the dark does not know where they are going."

Once Jesus left this world, He showed us how to stay in the light after He was gone—through the Holy Spirit. Jesus tells us again that He will offer us salvation. Through the gift of free will, we get to choose which path we will follow. Our choices are simple; either the narrow gate that is less traveled, or the wide gate, which we know is not a good option.

February 25 ____________________

Verse of the Day

JAMES 4:10

Humble yourself before the Lord, and he will lift you up.

Humility surely is something the world needs, starting with myself.

February 26 ______________________________

Verse of the Day

HEBREWS 10:26-27

If we deliberately keep sinning after we have received the knowledge of the truth, no sacrifice for sin is left, but only a fearful expectation of judgement and of raging fire that will consume the enemies of God.

How severe of a warning do we need? Most of my life I didn't know the Word. But once I educated myself and learned the message that Jesus left for us, I understood that I needed to change my life and listen to the warnings that were spelled out clearly in Scripture.

February 27 ______________________________

Verse of the Day

MATTHEW 8:26-27

He replied, "You of little faith, why are you so afraid?" Then he got up and rebuked the winds and the waves, and it was completely calm. The men were amazed and asked, "What kind of man is this? Even the winds and the waves obey him!"

The power of faith! Once we surrender ourselves to God and show faith in what Jesus tells us, nothing can overwhelm us. Life is hard; I couldn't imagine doing it without faith ever again. I tried that for a long time. I tried doing this world my way, and every step of the way darkness crept in. I now see it plainly; I know that darkness has lifted. Moreover, I now know the feeling of wearing the full armor of God to protect me.

February 28 ______________________________

Verse of the Day

MATTHEW 26:41

"Watch and pray so that you will not fall into temptation. The spirit is willing, but the flesh is weak."

Once you have surrendered yourself in the Lord, praying every day becomes deeply important, because temptation has a harder time infiltrating our life when we keep ourselves surrounded by God. As the saying goes, "you reap what you sow." If we invest nothing with the Lord, why should we expect something in return?

CHAPTER 3

March

THIS chapter begins with a verse that I consider extremely important!

March 4

Verse of the Day

1 THESSALONIANS 2:4

For we speak as messengers approved by God to be entrusted with the Good News. Our purpose is to please God, not people. He alone examines the motives in our hearts.

We may fool others, we may even fool ourselves, but I believe God knows our motives, and we will have to answer to Him, not the ones we might be trying to fool.

March 5

Verse of the Day

JOHN 7:17 NLT

Anyone who wants to do the will of God will know whether my teaching is from God or is merely my own.

If we are carrying out the will of God, we will feel God's presence and know the gift of His presence is not from any man.

March 8

Verse of the Day

JOHN 6:27

"Do not work for food that spoils, but work for food that endures to eternal life, which the Son of Man will give you. For on him God the Father has put his seal of approval."

March 10

Verse of the Day

LUKE 6:46-49

"Why do you call me 'Lord, Lord,' and do not what I say? As for everyone who comes to me and hears my words and puts them into practice, I will show you what they are like. They are like a man building a house, who dug down deep and laid a foundation on rock. When a flood came, the torrent struck that house but could not shake it, because it was well built. But the one who hears my words and does not put them to practice is like a man who built a house on ground without a foundation. The moment the torrent struck that house, it collapsed and its destruction was complete."

March 12 ______________________________

Verse of the Day

PSALM 62:1-2

Truly my soul finds rest in God; my salvation comes from him. Truly he is my rock and my salvation; he is my fortress, I will never be shaken.

When things get hard, I know God is always with me.

March 14 ______________________________

Verse of the Day

2 CORINTHIANS 5:17 NLT

Anyone who belongs to Christ has become a new person. The old life is gone; a new life has begun.

This is what it is to be born again. I now understand this verse, though I had to live it to fully understand it.

March 15

Verse of the Day

MARK 7:6-8

He replied, "Isaiah was right when he prophesied about you hypocrites; as it is written: 'These people honor me with their lips, but their hearts are far from me. They worship me in vain; their teachings are merely human rules.' You have let go of the commands of God and are holding on to human traditions."

Some say they are Christians, but they are merely mouthing the words. To be a true Christian, one must live one's life according to Jesus' teachings. The prevalence of hypocrites in many arenas of life is no reason not to be a follower of Jesus—it's an excuse. To honor Jesus is to have a personal relationship with Him, not a religion; it is to follow His teachings.

March 16

Verse of the Day

PROVERBS 14:15

The simple believe anything, but the prudent give thought to their steps.

We should take special heed to this verse. Today's society includes influencers from various walks of life—media, entertainment, education, politics—with impure motives attempting to get us to believe the opposite of what Jesus teaches us. This verse is a great warning to be prudent in our steps. We should thoroughly investigate what we believe!

March 22 ______________________

Verse of the Day

MATTHEW 6:22-23

"The eye is the lamp of the body. If the eyes are healthy, your whole body will be full of light. But if the eyes are unhealthy, your whole body will be full of darkness. If then the light within you is darkness, how great is that darkness!"

Guard what you allow yourself to watch, read, or take part in—it can destroy you from within. A saying in the technology world is "Good in, good out." If we allow bad content in it will fester. Conversely, if we allow only good content in it will spread.

March 23 ______________________

Verse of the Day

ROMANS 5:5

And hope does not put us to shame, because God's love has been poured out into our hearts through the Holy Spirit, who has been given to us.

God's amazing love is there for us to receive always! At this point, I would like to explain one of the biggest reasons I chose to compile *Verse of the Day* into a book. One of main reasons I wrote this book is so that my kids would read it. I didn't raise Deanna and Michael with a foundation rooted in God and Jesus. We did attempt briefly, but I put worldly activities ahead of spirituality. Knowing what I know now, I wish I had introduced them and guided them in a spiritual way of life.

Since they are now adults, they can make their own decisions. I hope that by living my life in a godly manner, I can be a good example of why they should make an effort to learn what I now see plainly. Since I fall short when I try to explain my journey to them, I hope that reading this book will help them find their way to God, or at least understand why I did. My hope is that they realize that we cannot live in this world on our own terms, and we cannot enter the next without following God's terms.

March 24 ________________________________

Verse of the Day

1 JOHN 3:24

The one who keeps God's commands lives in him, and he in them. And this is how we know that he lives in us. We know it by the Spirit he gave us.

It is not enough to *know* God's commands, we must *obey* them also. Many people who claim to be Christian still do not obey God. If that is you, try harder!

March 25 ____________________

Verse of the Day

PROVERBS 21:23

Those who guard their mouths and their tongues keep themselves from calamity.

Ask God for wisdom in your words; avoid arguments with fools who want to drag you down! This is also one of the devil's tactics. Have you heard the phrase "Sink to their level?" We cannot let that happen to us!

March 26 ____________________

Verse of the Day

2 CORINTHIANS 5:1

For we know that if the earthly tent we live in is destroyed, we have a building from God, an eternal house in heaven, not built by human hands.

I now know to make my investments into the Spirit rather than the world. God is the supernatural; there are no limits to what He can do in our lives. Our brains cannot grasp the concept of His power.

March 29 ______________________________

Verse of the Day

LUKE 24:7-8

"The Son of Man must be delivered over to the hand of the sinners, be crucified, and on the third day be raised again." Then they remembered his words.

Prophets predicted the crucifixion and many heard these words. It is hard for me to believe that so many still refuse to listen and believe. In my earlier life, I did not know the teachings of Jesus, having never been exposed to them, or taught them. But once I started to understand, research, and surrender myself to God, I never looked back. Thank You, God, for letting me see the light, for letting me escape the darkness. You had been offering this to me for so long but I was too blind, too caught up in this world to see or hear. Thank You!

March 30

Verse of the Day

JOHN 8:23-24

But he continued, "You are from below, I am from above. You are of this world; I am not of this world. I told you that you would die in your sins; if you do not believe that I am he, you will indeed die in your sins."

Even after endless miracles that were witnessed by countless people, many still question His sovereignty. He fulfilled many prophecies also with witnesses, yet many still question or just do not take the time to research and study. The biggest event in human history, the Resurrection, which so many have tried to disprove only to end up converting to believers themselves, and still so many ignore this event of such great magnitude. I hope we all take the time to understand the significance of Jesus Christ's time here on Earth.

CHAPTER 4

April

Ten Verses about Faith

MATTHEW 17:20 – *"Truly I tell you, if you have faith as small as a mustard seed, you can say to this mountain, 'Move from here to there,' and it will move. Nothing will be impossible for you."*

JOHN 7:38 – *"Whoever believes in me, as Scripture has said, rivers of living water will flow from within them."*

ROMANS 15:13 – *May the God of hope fill you with all joy and peace as you trust in Him, so that you may overflow with hope by the power of the Holy Spirit.*

JOHN 6:35 – *Then Jesus declared, "I am the bread of life. Whoever comes to me will never go hungry, and whoever believes in me will never be thirsty."*

ROMANS 10:9 – *If you declare with your mouth, "Jesus is Lord," and believe in your heart that God raised him from the dead, you will be saved.*

EPHESIANS 3:16-18 – *I pray that out of his glorious riches he may strengthen you with power through his Spirit in your inner being, so that Christ may dwell in your hearts through faith. And I pray that* *you, being rooted and established in love, may have power, together with all the Lord's holy people, to grasp how wide and long and high and deep is the love of Christ.*

GALATIANS 2:16 – *Know that a person is not justified by the works of the law, but by faith in Jesus Christ. So we, too, have put our faith in Christ Jesus that we may be justified by faith in Christ and not by the works of the law, because by the works of the law no one will be justified.*

GALATIANS 2:20 – *I have been crucified with Christ and I no longer live, but Christ lives in me. The life I now live in the body, I live by faith in the Son of God, who loved me and gave himself for me.*

1 PETER 1:21 – *Through him you believe in God, who raised him from the dead and glorified him, and so your faith and hope are in God.*

2 CORINTHIANS 5:7 – *For we live by faith, not by sight.*

April 1 ________________________

Verse of the Day

MATTHEW 7:24-27

"Therefore everyone who hears these words of mine and puts them into practice is like a wise man who built his house on rock. The rain came down, the streams rose, and the winds blew and beat against the house; yet it did not fall, because it had its foundation on the

rock. But everyone who hears these words of mine and does not put them into practice is like the foolish man who built his house on sand. The rain came down, the streams rose, and the winds blew and blew and beat against that house, and it fell with a great crash."

Where is *your* house built? Do you seek wisdom or intellect? So many warnings!

April 2 ___

Verse of the Day

JAMES 1-22-24

Do not merely listen to the word, and so deceive yourselves. Do what it says. Anyone who listens to the word but does not do what it says is like someone who looks at his face in the mirror and after looking at himself, goes away and immediately forgets what he looks like.

It's not good enough to just *read* the teachings of Jesus and the Scriptures of the Old Testament, we need to *apply* them to our everyday life. Many say they are believers, Christians, but never even open the Bible, or make an effort to learn what Jesus wants of us, or look at His instructions. To me, that is like saying, "I am a pilot, but never took the time to learn to fly."

April 3

Verse of the Day

PSALM 63:3-5

Because your love is better than life, my lips will glorify you. I will praise you as long as I live, and in your name I will lift up my hands. I will be fully satisfied as with the richest of foods; with singing lips my mouth will praise you.

An axiom that came to me when I first fully came to God was, "You can have everything and yet have nothing, and you can have nothing and yet have everything." When we have God and Jesus in our lives, we have everything!

April 6

Verse of the Day

JUDE 17-19

But, dear friends, remember what the apostles of our Lord Jesus Christ foretold. They said to you, "In the last times there will be scoffers who will follow their own ungodly desires." These are the people who divide you, who follow mere natural instincts and do not have the Spirit.

I will say it again. Be mindful of who and what you follow! The rest of the verse that follows (20-21) is the Good News, and the hope of our salvation.

JUDE 20-21

But you, dear friends, by building yourself up in your holy faith and praying in the Holy Spirit, keep yourselves in God's love as you wait for the mercy of our Lord Jesus Christ to bring you to eternal life.

April 7

Verse of the Day

PROVERBS 13:15

Good judgement wins favor, but the way of the unfaithful leads to their destruction.

April 8

Verse of the Day

LUKE 12:4-5

I tell you, my friends, do not be afraid of those who kill the body and after that can do no more. But I will show you whom you should fear: Fear him who, after your body has been killed, has the authority to throw you into hell. Yes, I tell you, fear him.

Too many fear what happens now, during this life, but they do nothing to prepare for what happens in the afterlife! God warns us but gives us free will. If we choose to ignore God, we will have only ourselves to blame.

April 9 ____________________

Verse of the Day

MARK 10:52

"Go," said Jesus, "your faith has healed you." Immediately he received his sight and followed Jesus along the road.

Faith! That is what Jesus is asking us to have. The miracles of Jesus were witnessed and well-documented by many, but still so many doubted Him then and still do today. It was faith that healed those in the Bible.

April 10 ____________________

Verse of the Day

2 PETER 2:18-21

For they mouth empty, boastful words and, by appealing to the lustful desires of the flesh, they entice people who are just escaping from those who live in error. They promise them freedom, while they themselves are slaves of depravity—for people are slaves to whatever has mastered them. If they have escaped the corruption of the world by knowing our Lord and Savior Jesus Christ and are again entangled in it and are overcome, they are worse off at the end than they were at the beginning. It would have been better for them not to have known it and then turn their backs on the sacred command that was passed on to them.

We are living in a time when leaders—or aspiring leaders—are promising everything! They try to entice people with the lures of this world, like money and power. Jesus tells us to be cautious of these people; they can lead us into entrapment with those lures.

April 11

Verse of the Day

ISAIAH 26:2-3

Open the gates that the righteous nations may enter, the nation that keeps faith. You keep in perfect peace those whose minds are steadfast, because they trust in you.

We must stay a nation of faith, and we want our leaders to demonstrate their faith. When faith is absent in our leaders, we must keep the faith ourselves. We have seen throughout history what happens to those civilizations that turn away from God.

April 15

Verse of the Day

ACTS 17:30-31

In the past God overlooked such ignorance, but now he commands all people everywhere to repent. For he has set a day when he will judge the world with justice by the man he has appointed. He has given proof of this to everyone by raising him from the dead.

April 18 ________________________________

Verse of the Day

ROMANS 2:13

For it is not those who hear the law who are righteous in God's sight, but those who obey the law who will be declared righteous.

It is not easy to always live the way God wants us to live, but the alternative is to disappoint God . . . something I am unwilling to do. So many profess to be Christian or religious, but don't even know the Scriptures, let alone try to live by them. My goal is to live every day by the teachings of Jesus the best I can, to have a personal relationship with God, through Jesus, and to ask for forgiveness whenever I fall short.

April 21 – Easter Sunday____________________

Verse of the Day

MARK 10:45

"For even the Son of Man did not come to be served, but to serve, and to give his life as a ransom for many."

While it is nice to celebrate today with bunnies and candy and Easter baskets, let us not forget that Easter is the celebration of the resurrection of our Lord and Savior Jesus Christ. Let us also make sure to teach our kids the true meaning of Easter. I thank you Jesus for the sacrifice you gave for us!

April 22 ______________________________

Verse of the Day

JOHN 12:26

"Whoever serves me must follow me; and where I am, my servants also will be. My Father will honor the one who serves me."

It is not enough to say, "Well, I'm a good person." Jesus made it very clear what we need to do to be saved in order to have eternal life.

April 24 ______________________________

Verse of the Day

PSALM 34:4-5

I sought the Lord, and he answered me; he delivered me from all my fears. Those who look to him are radiant; their faces are never covered with shame.

All I know is I am so thankful that I found my way to God through Jesus! What else I know is we can *all* have this relationship with God. He is waiting!

April 25 ________________________________

Verse of the Day

LUKE 11:9-10

"So I say to you: Ask and it will be given to you; seek and you will find; knock and the door will be opened to you. For everyone who asks receives; the one who seeks finds; and to the one who knocks, the door will be opened."

Our requests to God should begin with our actions. If we take the steps to seek out God, through Jesus, He will receive us, but only if we have taken those first steps.

April 28 ________________________________

Verse of the Day

PROVERBS 12:22

The Lord detests lying lips, but he delights in people who are trustworthy.

We may think we are getting away with a lie, but know we are not! Regardless of whether or not we are caught, do we want to do something that the Lord detests?

April 29 ____________________________

Verse of the Day

PROVERBS 2:12-15

Wisdom will save you from the ways of wicked men, from men whose words are perverse, who have left straight paths to walk in dark ways, who delight in doing wrong and rejoice in the perverseness of evil, whose paths are crooked and who are devious in their ways.

Proverbs are like an instruction manual for life. Stay in the Word of God and act accordingly!

CHAPTER 5

May

EVEN though I have heard this story many times, it never gets old. We do serve an amazing God! Let us start with the most recognized verse itself.

JOHN 3:16 NIV

For God so loved world that he gave his one and only Son, that whoever believes in him shall not perish, but have eternal life.

Tim Tebow's Shocking Story about John 3:16 "Coincidence" Goes Viral

A video of former NFL quarterback Tim Tebow recalls an amazing biblical 'coincidence' in his life is going viral on social media.

The story began when Tebow was in his college football years. In 2009 he was weeks away from competing in the National Championship game, which would be highly televised. Tebow said God led him to write scripture references in eye black under his eyes for all the world to see while he played.

In the video, Tebow goes on to say "The next six weeks leading up to the game I was really agonizing and contemplating what verse and God kept bringing up to my heart and my head John 3:16, which is the essence of our Christianity. It is the essence of our hope."

After winning the National Championship game, Tebow found out something incredible had happened during the game: 94 million people had Googled the verse John 3:16. "Honestly my first thought was 'How do 94 million people not know John 3:16?'" He went on to say "I was just so humbled by how big the God is that we serve."

But that's not where the story ends. Three years later, in 2012, Tebow was a Denver Bronco playing the Pittsburg Steelers in the playoffs. After the Broncos won, he headed into the post-game press conference when his public relations representative stopped him in his tracks.

"He says, 'Timmy, did you realize what happened?' I was like, 'Yeah, we just beat the Steelers. We're going to play the Patriots.' And he was like, 'No, do you realize what happened?'" Tebow shared. "He said, 'It's exactly three years later from the day that you wore John 3:16 under your eyes,'" Tebow continued. "I was like, 'Oh, that's really cool.'"

"He said, 'No, I don't think you realize what happened. During the game you threw for 316 yards, your yards per completion were 31.6, your yards per rush were 3.16, the broadcast ratings for the night were 31.6, and the time of possession was 31.06. During the game 91 million people googled John 3:16 and it's the number one trend on every platform.'"

"I was just standing there in the hallway about to do this press conference, thinking that night was about a football game. It really wasn't—we serve such a big God," he shared.

Tebow believes God did something miraculous that night. "The God that we serve is a God of miracles," he said. "I just have to be willing to step out and say, 'Here you go, God, I'm going to give you my fish and my loaves of bread,' and watch what he does with it."

Source: CBN *The Christian Perspective*

May 2

Verse of the Day

PSALM 33:12

Blessed is the nation whose God is the Lord the people he chose for for his inheritance.

Our religious freedom is worth fighting for. I proudly served this country for many reasons, one of which was to ensure our religious freedom as well as God-given freedoms.

May 4 ______________________________

Verse of the Day

JOHN 5:22-23

"Moreover, the Father judges no one but has entrusted all judgement to the Son, that all may honor the Son just as they honor the Father. Whoever does not honor the Son does not honor the Father, who sent him."

I pray in the name of the Father, the Son, and the Holy Spirit. Amen. If you are not honoring the Father though his Son, then you are dishonoring him. Think about that.

May 5 ______________________________

Verse of the Day

PSALM 37:8-9

Refrain from anger and turn from wrath; do not fret—it leads only to evil. For those who are evil will be destroyed, but those who hope in the Lord will inherit the land.

May 6

Verse of the Day

PROVERBS 13:20-21

Walk with the wise and become wise, for a companion of fools suffers harm. Trouble pursues the sinner, but the righteous are rewarded with good things.

I try always to be guarded about whom I associate with, and whom I trust. Being careful is not enough, though. I also spend time researching. Our pastor said yesterday, "Show me your friends and I'll show you your future." So true!

May 9

Verse of the Day

ACTS 2:16-21

No, this is what was spoken by the prophet Joel: "In the last days," God says, "I will pour out my Spirit on all people. Your sons and daughters will prophesy, your young men will see visions, your old men will dream dreams. Even on my servants, both men and women, I will pour out my Spirit in those day, and they will prophesy. I will show wonders in the heavens above and sighs on the earth below, blood and fire and billows of smoke. The sun will be turned to darkness and the moon to blood before the coming of the great and glorious day of the Lord. And everyone who calls on the name of the Lord will be saved."

For non-believers, why would you not want to study what Jesus spoke, for at least no other reason than to be sure of why you don't believe? God is offering us eternal life and yet so many don't even bother to look into this claim so as to make an informed decision. They think of themselves as intellectuals and yet have never read the best-selling book in history. Seems like such a big gamble!

May 10 ______________________________

Verse of the Day

1 PETER 3:8-9

Finally, all of you, be like-minded, be sympathetic, love one another, be compassionate and humble. Do not repay evil with evil or insult with insult. On the contrary, repay evil with blessing, because to this you were called so that you may inherit a blessing.

Can you imagine our world if everyone lived by the teachings of Jesus? Jesus forgave us our sins, so how can we *not* give forgiveness to those who hurt us?

May 11 ___

Verse of the Day

PSALM 37:1-3

Do not fret because of those who are evil or be envious of those who do wrong; for like the grass they will soon wither, like green plants they will soon die away. Trust in the Lord and do good; dwell in the land and enjoy safe pasture.

May 17 ___

Verse of the Day

COLOSSIANS 3:5-6

Put to death, therefore, whatever belongs to your earthly nature: sexual immorality, impurity, lust, evil desires, and greed, which is idolatry. Because of these, the wrath of God is coming.

We are warned repeatedly about evil traps throughout the Bible. Evil will try to separate us from God, beginning with small thoughts and temptations. Each time we succumb, we move further and further away from God. I try to live by the saying, "Just do the right thing." When things begin to get tough I try to remember that "I can do all things through Christ, who gives me strength"

May 18 ______________________________

Verse of the Day

1 PETER 4:18

If it is hard for the righteous to be saved, what will become of the ungodly and the sinner?

Being saved takes dedication and commitment! Jesus has shown us what He expects of us, but so many don't even care to know His words. It's like the old adage, "You can lead a horse to water, but you can't make him drink." If we know the Word at all, we know what will happen to the ungodly and the sinner. Why do so many turn away?

May 20 ______________________________

Verse of the Day

MATTHEW 13:47-51 NLT

"Again, the Kingdom of Heaven is like a fishing net that was thrown into the water and caught fish of every kind. When the net was full, they dragged it up onto the shore, sat down, and sorted the good fish into crates, but threw the bad ones away. That is the way it will be at the end of the world. The angels will come and separate the wicked people from the righteous, throwing the wicked into the fiery furnace, where there will be weeping and gnashing of teeth. Do you understand all these things?"

I love this verse, because it cannot be any more clearly spelled out! Harsh though it may seem, this verse tells us why it is important to *know* what is written and *live* by it. At the very least, knowing God's Word allows one to make informed decisions. Do you understand?

May 21 ______________________________

Verse of the Day

LUKE 11:2-4

Jesus said, "This is how you should pray. 'Father, hallowed be your name, your Kingdom come. Give us each day our daily bread, forgive us our sins, as we forgive those who sin against us. And lead us not into temptation.'"

Again I say, all God wants is a personal relationship with you. Speak with Him every day!

May 27 ______________________________

Verse of the Day

2 JOHN 1:9 NLT

Anyone that wanders away from this teaching has no relationship with God. But anyone that remains in the teaching of Christ has a relationship with both the Father and the Son.

It is easy to stray. What I have found is that if I am not in the Word every day, it is all too easy to fall into more of the earthly ways. Free will is tough; God wanted to leave salvation up to us.

May 29 ____________________

Verse of the Day

JOHN 20:29

Then Jesus told him, "Because you have seen me, you believe; blessed are those who have not seen me and yet have belief."

I choose faith! Others may choose to gamble and not believe, or create their own set of beliefs. Again, I choose faith! Thank You, Father!

May 30 ____________________

Verse of the Day

MATTHEW 17:5

While still speaking, a bright cloud covered them, and a voice from the cloud said, "This is my Son, whom I love; with him I am well pleased. Listen to him!"

Do we listen to him? Do we even bother to know him?

May 31 ______________________________

Verse of the Day

JOB 8:5-6

But if you will seek God earnestly and plead with the Almighty, if you are pure and upright, even now he will rouse himself on your behalf and restore you to your prosperous state.

God offers so much and all He asks of us is to seek an honest personal relationship with Him. I know I say it over and over again, but throughout the Bible God is trying to reach us before it's too late. He gives us so many opportunities to reach out for Him, but too many people either don't understand, don't take the time to try and understand, or just don't want to invest their time in understanding.

CHAPTER 6

June

I wanted to share some inspirational thoughts. Unfortunately, I don't know the source of some of them, while others I have written myself.

- Death can be your finish line or it can be your starting line to eternity!
- If you want to talk to God, you first have to believe you can hear from Him.
- Better to humble yourself, then to have God do it for you.
- God uses ordinary people to do extraordinary things.
- No matter what my situation is, I will have JOY, because I know I have salvation. Knowing this what can possibly ruin my JOY. It does not get any better than salvation!
- What unites us is greater than what divides us.
- Integrity is when your walk matches your talk.
- There are many ways to get to Hell, but only one way to get to Heaven.

Ten Verses about Deceit

TITUS 1:16 – *They profess to know God, but by their deeds they deny Him, being detestable and disobedient and worthless for any good deed.*

1 PETER 2:1 – *Therefore, put aside all malice and all deceit and hypocrisy and envy and all slander of every kind.*

2 CORINTHIANS 4:2 – *But we have renounced the things hidden because of shame, not walking in craftiness or adulterating the word of God, but by the manifestation of truth commending ourselves to every man's conscience in the sight of God.*

EPHESIANS 5:6 – *Let no one deceive you with empty words, for because of these things the wrath of God comes upon the sons of disobedience.*

PSALM 5:6 – *You destroy those who speak falsehood; the Lord abhors the man of bloodshed and deceit.*

MICAH 6:11 – *Can I justify wicked scales and a bag of deceptive weights?*

PROVERBS 12:17 – *He who speaks truth tells what is right, but a false witness, deceit.*

PROVERBS 14:5 – *A trustworthy witness will not lie, but a false witness utters lies.*

PROVERBS 19:9 – *A false witness will not go unpunished, and he who tells lies will perish.*

JOB 27:4 – *My lips certainly will not speak unjustly, nor will my tongue mutter deceit.*

June 1 ______________________________

Verse of the Day

PROVERBS 28:9

If anyone turns a deaf ear to my instruction even their prayers are detestable.

Just Wow!

June 2 ______________________________

Verse of the Day

ROMANS 14:10-12

You, then, why do you judge your brother or sister? Or why do you treat them with contempt? For we will all stand before God's judgement seat. It is written, 'As surely as I live, says the Lord, every knee will bow before me; every tongue will acknowledge God.' So then, each of us will give an account of ourselves to God.

We need to stop judging others! How about replacing judgement with love? Our final judgement will be based on whether we accepted Christ as our Lord and Savior, what kind of relationship we had with God, and how we learned and applied the teachings of Jesus! God knows what is in our hearts!

June 3 ______________________________

Verse of the Day

TIMOTHY 4:7-8

Have nothing to do with godless myths and old wise tales; rather, train yourself to be godly. For physical training is of some value, but godliness has value for all things, holding promise for both the present life and the life to come.

So many have time to workout but spend no time exercising spiritual training. I was one of them! I spent so much time trying to be the best at my job while making sure to get my exercise routine done every day; I trained in the military to make sure I was always prepared. Until I started my spiritual training, I never realized that I was missing the most important training of all. We need to check our priorities!

June 6 ______________________________

Verse of the Day

JOHN 15:5-6

"I am the vine; you are the branches, if you remain in me and I in you, you will bear much fruit; apart from me you can do nothing. If you do not remain in me, you are like a branch that is thrown away and withers; such branches are picked up, thrown into the fire and burned."

Jesus told us what He expects and told us what we should expect if we do not listen!

June 7 ____________________

Verse of the Day

JAMES 3:16

For where you have envy and selfish ambition, there you find disorder and every evil practice.

We see many people wanting power in both business and political arenas. This verse to me covers many areas of the world we live in, so we should be cautious in *all* areas, however it seems to be most prevalent in politics. Those who thirst for power exist around the world. It's good to question others' intentions.

June 8 ____________________

Verse of the Day

MATTHEW 24:12-14

Because of the increase of wickedness, the love of most will grow cold, but the one that stands firm to the end will be saved. And the gospel of the kingdom will be preached in the whole world as a testimony to all nations, and then the end will come.

As it is written, no one knows the time or day the Lord will return. My advice is to always be ready for that day! Moreover, the only way to do that is to learn the teachings of Jesus.

June 10________________________________

Verse of the Day

PROVERBS 2:7-8

He holds success in store for the upright, he is a shield to those whose walk is blameless, for he guards the course of the just and protects the way of the faithful ones.

To stay on the path referred to in this verse takes daily exercise in the Word and a steady commitment. Daily effort is not easy, but it is necessary. Habits and concepts of great value are rarely easy to obtain, but having the power and protection of God with us is worth more than any worldly things we could ever strive to obtain.

June 11________________________________

Verse of the Day

1 CORINTHIANS 2:14 NLT

But people who aren't Spiritual can't receive these truths from God's Spirit. It all sounds foolish to them and they can't understand it, for only those who are Spiritual can understand what the Spirit means.

This to me is just common sense. Once we experience the feeling of the Holy Spirit, we want to know more and more, but our own individual surrender is what helps us understand. There are no words to describe it.

June 12

Verse of the Day

1 PETER 2:1-3

Therefore, rid yourself of all malice and all deceit, hypocrisy, envy, and slander of every kind. Like newborn babies, crave pure spiritual milk, so that by it you may grow up in your salvation, now that you have tasted that the Lord is good.

The only way to live in accordance with what God wants is to surrender to Him. First, we need to accept the Lord Jesus as our Savior, then learn to live by the words He provided. Once we do this, we understand His expectations and can develop our own, never looking back.

June 13

Verse of the Day

JAMES 1:5-8 NLT

If you need wisdom, ask our God, and he will give it to you. He will not rebuke you for asking. But when you ask him, be sure that your faith is in God alone. Do not waiver, for a person with divided loyalty is as unsettling as a wave of the sea that is blown and tossed by the wind. Such a person should not expect to receive anything from the Lord. Their loyalty is divided between God and the world, and they are unstable in everything they do.

If we are asking and not receiving, it may be because we are not following what God is asking!

June 20

Verse of the Day

MARK 7:6-7

"Isaiah was right when he prophesied about you hypocrites; as it is written: These people honor me with their lips, but their hearts are far from me. They worship me in vain; their teachings are merely human rules."

God knows your heart, you may think you are fooling others around you but God will always be able to weigh your heart.

June 22

Verse of the Day

TITUS 3:10-11

Warn a divisive person once, and then warn them a second time. After that, have nothing to do with them. You may be sure that such a people are warped and sinful; they are self-condemned.

Not only do I choose, but also it is written "to avoid people that are intent on dividing others." We see this everywhere today, as we are living in a time that divisive tactics and labelling of others are at epidemic proportions. We should not be divided by titles like Man or Woman, Race, Straight, Gay, or any other term of sexuality. Nor should we be segregated by Rich or Poor (class warfare), Republican or Democrat. Labels such as these are used by sinful people to pitch brother against brother, sister against sister. We are all made in the image of God! We are all brothers and sisters in Christ, and we should all just love one another as God commanded us to do, regardless of those with evil intent who divide us.

June 23____________________________________

Verse of the Day

JOHN 6:35

Then Jesus declared, "I am the bread of life. Whoever comes to me will never go hungry, and whoever believes in me will never be thirsty."

Do we understand what Jesus is offering us? We cannot discount the meaning of these words without investing time to understand fully what Jesus is telling us.

June 24

Verse of the Day

PSALM 119:33-35

Teach me, Lord, the way of your decrees, that I may follow it to the end. Give me understanding, so that I may keep your law and obey it with all my heart. Direct me in the path of your commands, for there I find delight.

Ask and you shall receive! The journey starts with our personal relationship with God, obedience to what He asks of us, and then asking for what we need. We need to keep in mind, however, that we must first do our part.

June 27

Verse of the Day

PROVERBS 10:24

What the wicked dread will overtake them; what the righteous desire will be granted.

The Book of Proverbs is such a great guide for navigating through this life. The Bible has the answers that we are all looking for; we just need to make the effort to find them.

CHAPTER 7

July

EVERY morning I read a message sent from Joel Osteen via email, called *Today's Word with Joel and Victoria.* Developing this habit is one of the methods I used on my journey early on, teaching me to put God first. This was today's post on 7/31/19 and I thought it was a valuable message worth sharing.

Today's Scripture

2 CORINTHIANS 12:9, NLT

Each time he said, "My grace is all you need. My power works best in weakness." So now I am glad to boast about my weaknesses, so that the power of Christ can work through me.

The Real You

WE live in a society that stresses image. It is common to go through life trying to impress people, to show them that we are strong, that we have it all together. Although it is good to carry ourselves with confidence, sometimes in our need to maintain our image, we wear a mask and pretend. We do not want anyone to see our weaknesses, our struggles, and our lack of answers. Scripture says that if we wear masks, God's power will not show up. God will not bless the ideal you, the pretend you, the future you; He is looking for the *real* you.

Remember that there is power in vulnerability. When we empty ourselves out, God can fill us. But being full of one's self—acting, pretending, keeping up one's image—allows no room for God. If we humble ourselves and get real, God will help us grow.

A Prayer for Today

"FATHER, thank You that I don't have to hide my weaknesses or mask my shortcomings. Thank You that Your power goes to work in me when I get real and honest. I humbly admit that I don't have it all together, but I'm glad You're still working on me. In Jesus' Name, Amen."

July 2

Verse of the Day

ACTS 5:38-39 NLT

So my advice is, leave these men alone. Let them go, if they are planning and doing these things merely on their own, it will soon be overthrown. But if it is from God, you will not be able to overthrow them. You may even find yourself fighting against God!

This was a Jewish leader's advice about the apostles John and Peter and their preaching of Jesus. We have seen how their message has spread across the world. Had their message been merely from men, Jesus' words would have faded away, but we see that is not what happened. Really take the time to think about this verse!

July 7 ______________________________

Verse of the Day

PSALM 37:27-28

Turn from evil and do good; then you will dwell in the land forever. For the Lord loves the just and will not forsake his faithful ones.

Evil tries to creep into our lives in small ways; we have to be on guard at all times, in faith always, and in the Word daily. God will provide His armor of protection, but only if we do our part.

July 8 ______________________________

Verse of the Day

REVELATION 22:20-21

He who testifies to these things says, "Yes, I am coming soon." Amen, come, Lord Jesus. The grace of the Lord Jesus be with God's people. Amen.

These are the last verses in the Bible. Can we be confident that we have a relationship with God, through his Son, Jesus?

July 9 ________________________________

Verse of the Day

MARK 8:27-29

Jesus and his disciples went on to the villages around Caesarea Philippi, on the way he asked them, "Who do people say I am?" They replied, "Some say you are John the Baptist; others say Elijah; and still others, one of the prophets." "But what about you? Who do you say I am?" Peter answered, "You are the Messiah."

I am so happy that I know who Jesus is, and I know that it is through Him that I have a relationship with God and salvation.

July 10________________________________

Verse of the Day

1 CORINTHIANS 2:9-10

However, as it is written, "What no eye has seen, what no ear has heard, and what no human mind has conceived" the things God has prepared for those who love him—these are the things God has revealed to us by his Spirit.

God has given us the opportunity over and over again to have a relationship with Him through His son Jesus Christ. Now we have the choice to do what he ask of us! Choose wisely!

July 11____________________________________

Verse of the Day

ACTS 5:29

Peter and the other apostles replied: "we must obey God rather than human beings!"

This is simple, and unfortunately often forgotten. Too many have become too lazy to teach or learn. People spend more time in their fantasy football league or other such pastimes than they do studying the Bible.

July 12____________________________________

Verse of the Day

2 TIMOTHY 2:11-13

Here is a trustworthy saying: If we died with him; we will also live with him; if we endure, we will also reign with him. If we disown him, he will also disown us; if we are faithless, he remains faithful, for he cannot disown himself.

July 14______________________________

Verse of the Day

2 TIMOTHY 3:1-5

But mark this: There will be terrible times in the last days. People will be lovers of themselves, lovers of money, boastful, proud, abusive, disobedient to their parents, ungrateful, unholy, without love, unforgiving, slanderous, without self-control, brutal, not lovers of good, treacherous, rash, conceited, lovers of pleasure rather than of God—having a form of godliness but denying its power. Have nothing to do with these people.

We have free will, so if we see "these people" around us, we have the choice to turn away, no matter the cost or consequence. Nothing can equal the consequence of associating with those God warned us about in this verse.

July 15______________________________

Verse of the Day

PSALM 40:4

Blessed is the one who trusts in the Lord, who does not look to the proud, to those who turn aside to false gods.

July 22

Verse of the Day

PHILIPPIANS 2:3-5

Do nothing out of selfish ambition or vain conceit. Rather, in humility value others above yourselves, not looking to your own interest but each of you to the interest of others. In your relationship with one another, have the same mindset as Christ Jesus.

Love thy neighbor; love thy brother and sister and be humble! We are all neighbors and we are all brothers and sisters in Christ. Do not let anything divide us from one another! There are and always will be powers seeking to divide us through hate, deception, and lies. These attempts come from evil, not from God, because God is love.

July 24

Verse of the Day

EPHESIANS 6:10-11

Finally, be strong in the Lord and his mighty power. Put on the full armor of God, so that you can take your stand against the devil's schemes.

I posted this again because last night we watched a movie called, *Heaven's War.* I recommend this movie to anyone who wants to understand the true war in which we are involved.

July 25

Verse of the Day

PROVERBS 12:25

Anxiety weighs down the heart, but a kind word cheers it up.

July 26

Verse of the Day

JAMES 3-13-16

Who is wise and understanding among you? Let them show it by their good life, by deeds done in humility that comes from wisdom. But if you harbor bitter envy and selfish ambition in your hearts, do not boast about it or deny the truth. Such 'wisdom' does not come down from heaven but is earthly, unspiritual, demonic. For where you have envy and selfish ambition, there you will find disorder and every evil practice.

It's very simple—we need to make sure we are doing the right things for the right reasons. We must not overestimate our knowledge, if it is without heavenly wisdom!

July 27

Verse of the Day

REVELATION 11:15

The seventh angel sounded his trumpet, and there were loud voices in heaven, which said: "The kingdom of the world has become the kingdom of our Lord and of his Messiah, and he will reign for ever and ever."

So many want to take the chance to follow their own beliefs based on worldly practices, instead of the Word that has been passed down to us and inspired by God. If you study the prophets, so much of what they predicted has already come true. This is a big one—are you willing to chance that this prediction won't happen?

July 28

Verse of the Day

ISAIAH 55:6-7

Seek the Lord while he may be found; call on him while he is near. Let the wicked forsake their ways and the unrighteous their thoughts. Let them turn to the Lord, and he will have mercy on them, and to our God, for he will freely pardon.

God's offer is not available forever. Don't miss it!

July 29

Verse of the Day

1 CORINTHIANS 13:4-7

Love is Patient, love is kind. It does not envy, it does not boast, it is not proud. It does not dishonor others, it is not self-seeking, it is not easily angered, it keeps no record of wrongs. Love does not delight in evil but rejoices in truth. It always protects, always trusts, always hopes, always perseveres.

I am so happy that I have a relationship with a God full of Love. If what we follow is not rooted in Love then it is not from God, because He is Love!

July 30

Verse of the Day

PROVERBS 3:25-26

Have no fear of sudden disaster or of the ruin that overtakes the wicked, for the Lord will be at your side and will keep your foot from being snared.

Once we humble ourselves before the Lord, we can be on the path of contentment and true peace. Fears no longer exists. If this sounds repetitive, it is—so is God's message. He is just waiting for us to listen.

July 31

Verse of the Day

2 TIMOTHY 1:7

For the Spirit God gave us does not make us timid, but gives us power, love, and self-discipline.

I lacked the strength or discipline to fight and overcome my addictions and temptations until I humbled myself before the Lord Jesus and He filled me with the Holy Spirit. We can only know this feeling once we make that commitment! Thank You, God!

CHAPTER 8

August

AS parents we want the best for our children, we have so much love for them that we want to make sure all of their needs are met. As a father, I experienced a love that I never known before having children. I wanted to expand on this next verse from Luke because it made me really think, that if I want the very best for my children, having this amazing love for them, can I just imagine what God, our Father wants for us? What I understand now, he is just waiting for us to ask!

LUKE 11:11-13

"Which of you fathers, if your son asks for a fish, will give him a snake instead? Or if he asks for an egg, will give him a scorpion? If you then, though you are evil, know how to give good gifts to your children, how much more will your Father in heaven give the Holy Spirit to those who ask him!"

Ten Verses about Forgiveness

We Should Forgive Others as God Forgives Us

EPHESIANS 4:31-32 – *Get rid of all bitterness, rage and anger, brawling and slander, along with every form of malice. Be kind to one another, tenderhearted, forgiving one another, as God in Christ forgave you.*

MARK 11:25 – *And whenever you stand praying, forgive, if you have anything against anyone, so that your Father also who is in heaven may forgive you your trespasses."*

COLOSSIANS 3:13 – *Bearing with one another and, if one has a complaint against another, forgiving each other; as the Lord has forgiven you, so you also must forgive.*

MATTHEW 6:12 – *From the Lord's Prayer– "And forgive us our debts, as we also have forgiven our debtors."*

ROMANS 12:18-21 – *If possible, so far as it depends on you, live peaceably with all. Beloved, never avenge yourselves, but leave it to the wrath of God, for it is written, "Vengeance is mine, I will repay," says the Lord. To the contrary, if your enemy is hungry, feed him; if he is thirsty, give him something to drink; for by so doing you will heap burning coals on his head. Do not be overcome by evil, but overcome evil with good.*

MATTHEW 5:39-41 – *"But I tell you not to resist an evil person. If someone slaps you on your right cheek, turn to him the other also; if someone wants to sue you and take your tunic, let him have your cloak as well, and if someone forces you to go one mile, go with him two."*

PROVERBS 17:9 – *Love prospers when a fault is forgiven, but dwelling on it separates close friends.*

LUKE 6:35-36 – *"But love your enemies, do good to them, and lend to them without expecting to get anything back. Then your reward will be great, and you will be children of the Most High, because he is kind to the ungrateful and wicked. Be merciful, just as your Father is merciful."*

PROVERBS 10:12 – *Hatred stirs old quarrels, but love overlooks insults.*

JOHN 14:26-27 – *"But the Advocate, the Holy Spirit, whom the Father will send in my name, will teach you all things and will remind you of everything I have said to you. Peace I leave with you; my peace I give you. I do not give to you as the world gives. Do not let your hearts be troubled and do not be afraid."*

August 1 ______________________________

Verse of the Day

JOHN 12:47-48

"If anyone hears my words but does not keep them, I do not judge that person. For I did not come to judge the world, but to save the world. There is a judge for the one that rejects me and does not accept my words; the very words I have spoken will condemn them at the last day."

Take time to understand these words. To reject what Jesus was teaching is unimaginable to me now, but it took almost a lifetime for me to understand that.

August 3 ________________________________

Verse of the Day

PROVERBS 8:10-11

Choose my instruction instead of silver, knowledge rather than choice of gold, for wisdom is more precious than rubies, and nothing you desire can compare with her.

So many people think knowledge is solely based on their education. Knowledge without wisdom from God is of little value. We can find His instructions for wisdom in the Bible, along with how to have a personal relationship with Him through Jesus Christ! Seek and you will find.

August 4 ________________________________

Verse of the Day

JOHN 12:40

"He has blinded their eyes and hardened their hearts, so they can neither see with their eyes, nor understand with their hearts, nor turn—and I would heal them."

Once we turn to Jesus, He will give us the understanding. Every day we see and hear things that make us ask ourselves, "how can that person do that or think that?" Most likely, that person has no relationship with God, through Jesus, and his eyes are blinded and his heart is hardened.

Additional Verse

1 PETER 1:24-25

For all people are like grass, and all their glory is like the flowers of the field; the grass withers and the flowers fall, but the word of the Lord endures forever.

You will never truly understand this until you know the Word and it lives inside you. In good times or bad times, knowing that God is always with us is the best feeling imaginable.

August 5 ______________________________

Verse of the Day

HEBREWS 13:5-6

Keep your lives free from love of money and be content with what you have, because God has said, "Never will I leave you; never will I forsake you." So we say with confidence, "The Lord is my helper, I will not be afraid. What can mere mortals do to me?"

Once we understand God's message and humbly surrender ourselves to Him, it is only then that the weight of this world will be lifted from us. I believe then and only then can we experience true contentment. If true contentment is what you desire, you are obliged to make the first move. His door is always open.

August 8 ________________________

Verse of the Day

1 PETER 3:9

Do not repay evil with evil or insult with insult. On the contrary, repay evil with blessing, because to this you were called so that you may inherit blessing.

August 9

Verse of the Day

LUKE 10:27

He answered, "Love the Lord your God with all your heart and with all your soul and with all your strength and with all your mind, and love your neighbor as yourself."

Are we doing what God asked of us? Helping to change this world and achieve peace starts with this question.

August 11 ________________________

Verse of the Day

LUKE 11:17

Jesus knew their thoughts and said to them: "Any kingdom divided against itself will be ruined, and a house divided against itself will fall."

Evil divides us; we should not be fooled by divisive tactics. We need to check ourselves . . . if we are engaging in labeling others or supporting any individual or group that attempts to turn one against another we need to remember that this is a tactic used by evil forces. Those with impure motives would love to see our country fall. Terms like "fundamental transformation" should raise a red flag. That means to change from the root, the foundation. Those who use this phrase "fundamental transformation" mean to achieve their goal by dividing and conquering. These are evil and dangerous tactics.

August 12

Verse of the Day

MATTHEW 5:14-16

"You are the light of the world. A town built on the hill cannot be hidden. Neither do the people light a lamp and put it under a bowl. Instead they put it on a stand, and it gives light to everywhere in the house. In the same way, let your light shine before others, that they may see your good deeds and glorify your Father in heaven."

We do not want to hide our love for God and our dedication to Jesus. Rather, we want to let it shine so we can be a beacon for others, and in doing so please God. Who cares what people say or think? I care more about what God thinks.

August 16

Verse of the Day

MARK 12:28-31

One of the teachers of the law came and heard them debating. Noticing that Jesus had given them a good answer, he asked him, "Of all the commandments, which is the most important?" "The most important one," answered Jesus, "is this: Hear, O Israel: The Lord our God, the Lord is one. Love the Lord your God with all your heart and with all your soul and with all your mind and with all your strength. The second is this: Love your neighbor as yourself. There are no commandments greater than these."

We seem to be living in a time when people, organizations, and media are trying to influence others to defy the two most important commandments in God's eyes. We must not allow others to build hate for our neighbor or any person or group because of a difference in political beliefs or trivial matters.

August 17

Verse of the Day

PSALM 64:1-4

Hear me, my God, as I voice my complaint; protect my life from the threat of the enemy. Hide me from the conspiracy of the wicked, from the plots of the evildoers. They sharpen their tongues like swords and aim cruel words like deadly arrows. They shoot from ambush at the innocent; they shoot suddenly, without fear.

Those who do not bother to study the Word will not know how to face evil when it appears in their lives.

August 18____________________________________

Verse of the Day

2 TIMOTHY 1:3

I thank the God whom I serve, as my ancestors did, with clear conscience, as night and day I constantly remember you in my prayers.

This is how I have a personal relationship with God and I am so thankful for it!

August 19____________________________________

Verse of the Day

JOHN 16:12-13

"I have much more to say to you, more than you can bear. But when he, the Spirit of truth, comes, he will guide you into all truth. He will not speak on his own; he will speak only what he hears, and he will tell you what is yet to come."

This was Jesus' promise before He left us. If you have not received the Holy Spirit, it's because you have not asked or taken the time to learn how. I can only say it is an amazing gift! Thank You, God for opening my eyes!

August 20__________________________________

Verse of the Day

1 CORINTHIANS 3:18-20

Do not deceive yourselves. If any of you think you are wise by the standards of this age, you should become 'fools' so that you may become wise. For the wisdom of this world is foolishness in God's sight. As it is written: 'He catches the wise in their craftiness' and again, 'The Lord knows that the thoughts of the wise are futile.'

We seem to be living in a time when people arrogantly think they are superior in intelligence merely from the education they receive. We will never have true wisdom if we have not humbled ourselves before God!

August 21__________________________________

Verse of the Day

MATTHEW 19:16-17

Just then a man came up to Jesus and asked, "Teacher, what good thing must I do to get eternal life?" "Why do you ask me about what is good?" Jesus replied. "There is only one that is good. If you want to enter life, keep the commandments."

You must first know the Commandments to keep them! God gave us free will, so how we live our lives is our choice and our choice only. We need to choose wisely!

MOSES summoned all Israel and said:

Hear, O Israel, the decrees and laws I declare in your hearing today. Learn them and be sure to follow them. The LORD our God made a covenant with us at Horeb. It was not with our fathers that the LORD made this covenant, but with us, with all of us who are alive here today. The LORD spoke to you face to face out of the fire on the mountain. (At that time I stood between the LORD and you to declare to you the word of the LORD, because you were afraid of the fire and did not go up the mountain.) And he said:

"I am the LORD your God, who brought you out of Egypt, out of the land of slavery.

First Commandment

"You shall have no other gods before me."

Second Commandment

"You shall not make for yourself an idol in the form of anything in heaven above or on the earth beneath or in the waters below. You shall not bow down to them or worship them; for I, the LORD your God, am a jealous God, punishing the children for the sin of the fathers to the third and fourth generation of those who hate me, but showing love to a thousand generations of those who love me and keep my commandments."

Third Commandment

"You shall not misuse the name of the LORD your God, for the LORD will not hold anyone guiltless who misuses his name."

Fourth Commandment

"Observe the Sabbath day by keeping it holy, as the LORD your God has commanded you. Six days you shall labor and do all your work, but the seventh day is a Sabbath to the LORD your God. On it you shall not do any work, neither you, nor your son or daughter, nor your manservant or maidservant, nor your ox, your donkey, or any of your animals, nor the alien within your gates, so that your manservant and maidservant may rest, as you do. Remember that you were slaves in Egypt and that the LORD your God brought you out of there with a mighty hand and an outstretched arm. Therefore the LORD your God has commanded you to observe the Sabbath day."

Fifth Commandment

"Honor your father and your mother, as the LORD your God has commanded you, so that you may live long and that it may go well with you in the land the LORD your God is giving you."

Sixth Commandment

"You shall not murder."

Seventh Commandment

"You shall not commit adultery."

Eighth Commandment

"You shall not steal.

Ninth Commandment

"You shall not give false testimony against your neighbor.

Tenth Commandment

"You shall not covet your neighbor's wife. You shall not set your desire on your neighbor's house or land, his manservant or maidservant, his ox or donkey, or anything that belongs to your neighbor."

August 22

Verse of the Day

REVELATION 11:17

We give thanks to you, Lord God Almighty, the One who is and who was, because you have taken your great power and have begun to reign.

I do thank You, Lord. I choose to prepare myself for what is to come.

August 23

Verse of the Day

MATTHEW 15:17-19

Don't you see that whatever enters the mouth goes into the stomach and then out of the body? But the things that come out of a person's mouth come from the heart, and these defile them. For out of the heart comes evil thoughts—murder, adultery, sexual immorality, theft, false testimony, slander.

August 24

Verse of the Day

PSALM 94:21-22

The wicked band together against the righteous and condemn the innocent to death. But the Lord has become my fortress, and my God the rock in whom I take refuge.

God gives us everything we need to live in this world! Without His gifts, life is very difficult. All we have to do is accept Him.

August 25____

Verse of the Day

1 CORINTHIANS 2:12

What we have received is not the spirit of the world, but the Spirit who is from God, so that we may understand what God has freely given us.

We live in a time when so many have walked away from faith, question it, or never took the time to try and find it. The awe-inspiring experience of being filled by the Holy Spirit is difficult for me to describe. Anyone who wants to have this experience will have to surrender and commit themselves to ever understand that feeling.

Additional Verse

JOHN 1:29-34

The next day John saw Jesus coming toward him and said, "Look, the Lamb of God, who takes away the sin of the world! This is the one I meant when I said, a man who comes after me has surpassed me because he was before me. I myself did not know him, but the reason I came baptizing with water was that he might be revealed to Israel."

Then John gave this testimony: "I saw the Spirit come down from heaven as a dove and remain on him. And I myself did not know him, but the one who sent me to baptize with water told me, 'The man on whom you see the Spirit come down and remain is the one who will baptize with the Holy Spirit. I have seen and I testify that this is God's Chosen One.'"

This is such a powerful verse! Prophets spoke of this, people witnessed this, and scribes recorded this. Why would you not want to know more?

August 26___________________________

Verse of the Day

JOHN 3:3 NLT

Jesus replied, "I tell you the truth, unless you are born again, you cannot see the Kingdom of God."

Very simple and straightforward—we can ignore this now, but one day we will have to address it, and by then it may be too late. If you have not accepted God into your life, you are not prepared for what is yet to come.

August 30___________________________

Verse of the Day

JOHN 6:63-65

The Spirit gives life; the flesh counts for nothing. The words I have spoken to you—they are full of the Spirit and life. Yet there are some of you who do not believe. For Jesus had known from the beginning which of them did not believe and who would betray him. He went on to say, "This is why I told you that no one can come to me unless the Father enabled them."

If even after studying Jesus' teaching, someone were not to believe, it seems like it would be a likely choice to do research to prove *why* he does not believe. The decision to surrender is the most important decision of not just *our* life but also the lives of our children. We should not be influenced away from the gifts that Jesus promised based on what others tell us or anxiety about what others will think.

August 31

Verse of the Day

JOHN 17:9-11

I pray for them. I am not praying for the world, but for those you have given me, for they are yours. All I have is yours, and all you have is mine. And all glory has come to me through them. I will remain in the world no longer, but they are still in the world, and I am coming to you. Holy Father, protect them by the power of your name, the name you gave me, so that they may be one as we are one.

Jesus came to save those that will follow Him. God came to Earth to give us a chance to live in eternity with Him. We have to ask ourselves, is this important enough to invest our time to understand, to research, and to make sure beyond a shadow of a doubt that we either believe or don't believe?

CHAPTER 9

September

Why do people not want to know more about Jesus and his teachings?

IT has occurred to me that there may be several reasons why people don't want to know more about Jesus and His time on Earth. The time Jesus spent teaching has had the biggest impact on civilization—more so than any other event or person in our history. I started wondering, *once we do understand what is at stake, how can anyone just turn the other way?*

I'm not trying to offend anyone with my opinion, but I think this is important question that needs honesty in answering it. Below are some reasons I believe people don't want to know more about Jesus.

1. People are too lazy to invest the time to learn more.
2. People just listen to the naysayers and don't bother educating themselves so they can make an educated decision.
3. People just think, *Well, I'm a good person and if God is a good God I'll be all right.* If people would take the

time to learn what the Bible says, they would know it takes more than that.

4. People are more concerned about what is happening in this world and their own lives. They are not thinking about what is going to happen after our short time here on this earth. So many people are so self-consumed with things like their appearance, their possessions, what other think about them, their job status, or their status in general.
5. They just don't believe, maybe that is how they were raised or they have other beliefs or they have never been exposed to even thinking about Jesus.
6. They are embarrassed to admit their beliefs or to come out to their peers. They don't want to be that "religious guy."
7. They like their lifestyle—partying, drinking, and sexual encounters, among other activities.

This is another possible reason that many don't think about.

Some people are afraid to know more about Jesus! What if they study the facts and conclude Jesus was God on Earth? This would drastically change their lives. Upon knowing, you have to make some very big changes. Your old way of living life has to fade away or at the very least has to be drastically altered. Unless in the rare occurrence you were already living a Christ-like life.

Here are just a few things Jesus taught. Once we become born again, these are some of the things Jesus requires of us.

1. Be selfless; put others first and be like a servant; serve others as Jesus did.
2. Be humble; put God first before all else.
3. Be generous; give your best to God—He wants to see that your faith is strong and that you trust Him. This includes your finances as well as your time.
4. Surrender yourself to Him.
5. Confess your sins to God.
6. Repent of your sins.
7. Love your neighbor.
8. The only way to the Father is through the Son.

To do what Jesus taught takes commitment, faith, discipline, love, and more. I can say from experience though, it is worth anything we have to do!

Ten Verses on Being Thankful

1 CHRONICLES 16:34

"Give thanks to the Lord, for he is good; his love endures forever."

1 CHRONICLES 16:35

"Cry out, 'Save us, God our Savior; gather us and deliver us from the nations, that we may give thanks to your holy name, and glory in your praise.'"

EZRA 3:11

"With praise and thanksgiving they sang to the Lord: "He is good; his love toward Israel endures forever." And all the people gave a great shout of praise to the Lord, because the foundation of the house of the Lord was laid."

PSALM 7:17

"I will give thanks to the Lord because of his righteousness; I will sing the praises of the name of the Lord Most High."

PSALM 69:30

"I will praise God's name in song and glorify him with thanksgiving."

PSALM 95:2

"Let us come before him with thanksgiving and extol him with music and song."

PSALM 100:4

"Enter his gates with thanksgiving and his courts with praise; give thanks to him and praise his name."

JEREMIAH 30:19

"From them will come songs of thanksgiving and the sound of rejoicing. I will add to their numbers, and they will not be decreased; I will bring them honor, and they will not be disdained."

1 CORINTHIANS 1:4

"I always thank my God for you because of his grace given you in Christ Jesus."

1 CORINTHIANS 10:16

"Is not the cup of thanksgiving for which we give thanks a participation in the blood of Christ? And is not the bread that we break a participation in the body of Christ?"

September 2 ______________________________

Verse of the Day

ACTS 1:3

After his suffering, he presented himself to them and gave many convincing proofs that he was alive. He appeared to them over a period of forty days and spoke about the kingdom of God.

As I previously pointed out, hundreds of people witnessed seeing Jesus alive *after* He was crucified—He appeared to 500 people in just one place. The Resurrection is well documented. Research it for yourself!

September 3 ______________________________

Verse of the Day

PROVERBS 5:22-23

The evil deeds of the wicked ensnare them; the cords of their sins hold them fast. For lack of discipline they will die, led astray by their own great folly.

We cannot let sin get its grip on us. Insidious sinfulness edges into our lives in small ways at first, until we are deeply ensnared.

September 4 ______________________________

Verse of the Day

ACTS 26:17-18

I will rescue you from your own people and from the Gentiles. I am sending you to them to open their eyes and turn from the darkness to the light, and from the power of Satan to God, so that they may receive forgiveness of sins and a place among those who are sanctified by faith in me.

God uses unlikely people all throughout Scripture. One example is Paul, who had been a persecutor of Christians until he was selected by Jesus to spread His message.

September 5 ____________________

Verse of the Day

2 PETER 1:20-21

Above all, you must understand that no prophecy of the Scripture came about by the prophet's own interpretation of things. For prophecy never had its origin in the human will, but prophets, though human, spoke from God as they were carried along by the Holy Spirit.

The Bible has around 2000 predictions from the prophets and Jesus; to date so many of them have been fulfilled. Jesus was widely prophesied in the Old Testament and fulfilled many predictions before and during His time on Earth. Before you discount what is written, please take the time to learn it. It's easy to say you don't believe, what is hard is to explain why.

September 6 ____________________

Verse of the Day

PROVERBS 18:13

To answer before listening—that is folly and shame.

Our society used to rely on the Bible for guidance, and Proverbs is a book of wisdom and guidance. It is wise to study it. This verse reminds me of the saying, "God gave you two ears and one mouth, use them accordingly."

September 7 ______________________

Verse of the Day

1 PETER 3:10

For, whoever would love life and see good days must keep their tongue from evil and their lips from deceitful speech.

I try to think before I speak, because words *do* have consequences!

September 9 ______________________

Verse of the Day

LUKE 12:15

Then he said to them, "Watch out! Be on your guard against all kinds of greed; life does not consist in an abundance of possessions."

Simply put, we cannot be consumed by our possessions or for lust of things we want. Greed and coveting are tools of the devil, and we want to avoid evil in our life. As singer Bob Marley says, "Some people are so poor, all they have is money."

September 10 ______________________

Verse of the Day

JOEL 2:31-32

The sun will turn to darkness and the moon to blood before the coming of the great and dreadful day of the Lord. And everyone who calls on the name of the Lord will be saved; for on the Mount Zion in Jerusalem there will be deliverance as the Lord has said, even among the survivors whom the Lord calls.

Always remember we have been warned—both throughout the Bible and from our Lord Jesus Christ.

September 12 ______________________

Verse of the Day

ROMANS 12:2

Don't copy the behavior and customs of this world, but let God transform you into a new person by changing the way you think. Then you will learn to know God's will for you, which is good and pleasing and perfect.

Again, God gives us a choice. We get to choose whether we want to walk with God, have eternal life, be content, understand love, and so much more that He has promised us, or focus on worldly things and live with anxiety and fear.

September 13 ______________________

Verse of the Day

ROMANS 12:16

Live in harmony with one another. Do not be proud, but be willing to associate with people of low positions. Do not be conceited.

If the world could live by the teachings of Jesus, such a better world it would be.

September 14 ______________________

Verse of the Day

2 PETER 1:2-3

Grace and peace be yours in abundance through the knowledge of God and of Jesus our Lord. His divine power has given us everything we need for a godly life through our knowledge of him who called us by his own glory and goodness.

We can continue to measure knowledge through worldly studies or we can take the advice to measure it through spiritual studies. I choose the latter.

September 15

Verse of the Day

PROVERBS 14:14-15

The faithless will be fully repaid for their ways, and the good reward for theirs. The simple believe anything, but the prudent give thought to their steps.

I just love what has been written for our road map through this life. I choose to follow it, to be prudent!

September 16

Verse of the Day

1 CORINTHIANS 13:2-4

If I have a gift of prophecy and can fathom all mysteries and knowledge, and if I have a faith that I can move mountains, but do not have love, I am nothing. If I give all I possess to the poor and give over my body to hardship that I may boast, but do not have love, I gain nothing. Love is patient, love is kind. It does not envy, it does not boast, it is not proud. It does not dishonor others, it is not self-seeking, it is not easily angered, it keeps no record of wrongs.

If we allow ourselves in any way to be guided by hate, or find ourselves supporting groups that attempt to justify hateful actions, no matter what excuse we use to try to conceal them, we are displeasing God! We can never justify hate!

September 18 ______________________________

Verse of the Day

LUKE 17:1-2

Jesus said to his disciples: "Things that cause people to stumble are bound to come, but woe to anyone through whom they come. It would be better for them to be thrown into the sea with a millstone tied around their neck than to cause one of the little ones to stumble."

We must be careful what we teach to our youth. What we pass on to the next generation should be rooted in love, truth, and compassion. We cannot be the ones to make them stumble.

September 20 ______________________________

Verse of the Day

1 PETER 4:7-8

The end of all things is near. Therefore be alert and of sober mind so that you may pray. Above all, love each other deeply, because love covers a multitude of sins.

September 21 ______________________________

Verse of the Day

1 CORINTHIANS 15:33-34 NLT

Don't be fooled by those who say such things, for bad company corrupts good character. Think carefully about what is right, and stop sinning. For to your shame say that some of you don't know God at all.

It is our duty to be guarded about those we keep company with and where we get our beliefs. Show me your friends and I'll show you your future.

September 22 ______________________________

Verse of the Day

2 CORINTHIANS 3:16-18

But whenever someone turns to the Lord, the veil is taken away. For the Lord is the Spirit, and wherever the Spirit of the Lord is, there is freedom. So all of us who have had that veil removed can see and reflect the glory of the Lord. And the Lord—who is the Spirit—makes us more and more like him as we are changed into his glorious image.

This is how we take part in true freedom!

September 25 ______________________

Verse of the Day

MATTHEW 7:26-27

But everyone who hears these words of mine and does not put them into practice is like a foolish man who built his house on sand. The rain came down, the streams rose, and the winds blew and beat against that house, and it fell with a great crash.

What are you building the foundation of your life upon?

September 26 ______________________

Verse of the Day

JAMES 1:3

Because you know that the testing of your faith produces perseverance.

As our faith grows, we will be tested. The Bible talks about God pruning us so we will grow. If we are not strong enough to believe through the testing, how can we grow in our faith? Believing is easy when everything is going great, but can we stay in faith through those hard times? When we do, we really begin to see God's rewards.

CHAPTER 10

Apostles, Disciples, and Human Nature

I am going to take a break from the daily verses to share something that changed my thinking.

This thought was pointed out to me. Unfortunately, I cannot recall from what source, but I know that I need to share it. It expounded the concept that the apostles and disciples would have no reason to spread the narrative of the resurrection other than its being true.

The resurrection of Jesus remains one of the most pivotal points in either believing or not believing in Jesus, the New Testament, and His teachings. I offer the following observations, for these points have provided me with a clear response to any non-believer.

Eleven Apostles claimed to have seen Jesus resurrected. Every one of them went through extreme persecution and all but one suffered imprisonment and/or a brutal death. Now the first point: If the resurrection started out as a lie, so that the disciples would continue the teachings that Jesus taught them, how far do you think a group of common followers would be willing to take it?

The disciples witnessed their teacher, a man they loved, put to a brutal death, tortured, ridiculed, and crucified—a death they surely would not want to endure themselves. Do you think it likely all eleven apostles and the countless disciples would have stuck to a so-called story, a lie?

This brings me to human nature. I could see maybe a couple or even up to four or five willing to continue the story of the resurrection for their own purposes. But if you think all eleven would stick to the same story after their own persecution, torture, imprisonment, and threats of a brutal death were levied against them, then you might not know human nature. It would have only taken one of them saying it was a lie to put doubt in people's minds.

The point is, after Jesus was put to death, none of these men had anything to gain from continuing their quest to spread the words of Jesus—and had everything to lose—yet all of them did just that. All of them sacrificed everything they had, traveling as far as they could, suffering, and writing the New Testament, all in the name of Jesus. They had no motive to continue this narrative.

As J. Warner Wallace has noted in his lectures and books, when a conspiracy is formed there are three motivating factors behind such a move—power, greed, and/or lust. The disciples would hold no power behind claiming the resurrection as truth. They were running around while often being threatened by the Jewish and Roman authorities. As for greed, they taught that one should not desire earthly possessions, but spiritual ones. Lust was not a factor, either. They taught celibacy before marriage and marital fidelity after marriage. In fact, N.T. Wright notes in his classic book, *The Resurrection of the Son of God,* that the disciples had no theological motivation behind claiming that Jesus had risen from the dead, as they were anticipating a military hero and a final resurrection at the end of time. What motivating factors existed for these disciples to invent such a story? None! The only reason the disciples taught the resurrection of Jesus was because Jesus's resurrection had occurred.[1]

I mentioned the movie *The Case for Christ* earlier. I again suggest watching this movie and seeing for yourself the evidence Lee Strobel of *The Chicago Tribune* uncovered while trying to disprove the resurrection, only to realize that the facts are overwhelming. He went from being an atheist to now sharing his story around the world.

[1] Source- crossexamined.org

"Christianity, if false, is of no importance, and if true, of infinite importance. The only thing it cannot be is moderately important."

—C.S. Lewis

So why did the Apostles persist in their beliefs? Could it be that they truly witnessed God on Earth? That they understood that Jesus was offering us eternal life? Only something of this magnitude would keep them willing to do what they did.

My last point: If, knowing this, you still do not want to learn more of what Jesus was trying to tell us, then I just don't understand what it would take. I wanted to include what the apostles endured for us to know the Word!

Peter and Paul – were both martyred in Rome about 66 AD, during the persecution under Emperor Nero. Paul was beheaded. Peter was crucified, upside down at his request, since he did not feel he was worthy to die in the same manner as his Lord.

Andrew – went to the "land of the man-eaters," in what is now the Soviet Union. Christians there claim him as the first to bring the gospel to their land. He also preached in Asia Minor, modern-day Turkey, and in Greece, where he is said to have been crucified.

Thomas – was probably most active in the area east of Syria. Tradition has him preaching as far east as India, where the ancient Marthoma Christians revere him as their founder. They claim that he died there when pierced through with the spears of four soldiers.

Philip – possibly had a powerful ministry in Carthage in North Africa and then in Asia Minor, where he converted the wife of a Roman proconsul. In retaliation the proconsul had Philip arrested and cruelly put to death.

Matthew – the tax collector and writer of a gospel ministered in Persia and Ethiopia. Some of the oldest reports say he was not martyred, while others say he was stabbed to death in Ethiopia.

Bartholomew – had widespread missionary travels attributed to him by tradition: to India with Thomas, back to Armenia, and also to Ethiopia and Southern Arabia. There are various accounts of how he met his death as a martyr for the gospel.

James – the son of Alpheus is one of at least three Jameses referred to in the New Testament. There is some confusion as to which is which, but this James is reckoned to have ministered in Syria. The Jewish historian Josephus reported that he was stoned and then clubbed to death.

Simon the Zealot – so the story goes, ministered in Persia and was killed after refusing to sacrifice to the sun god.

Matthais – the apostle chosen to replace Judas. Tradition sends him to Syria with Andrew and to death by burning.

John – The only one of the apostles generally thought to have died a natural death from old age. He was the leader of the church in the Ephesus area and is said to have taken care of Mary, the mother of Jesus, in his home. During Domitian's persecution in the middle '90s, he was exiled to the island of Patmos. There he is credited with writing the last book of the New Testament—the Revelation. An early Latin tradition has him escaping unscathed after being cast into boiling oil in Rome.

(The above account of the Apostles Source is found at Christianity.com)

CHAPTER 11

October

SO many people live with anxiety, fear, and worry. They try to take on the world alone, instead of realizing that God left the greatest tool of all to help us not just get by, but to thrive. We can continue trying to do it our way, or we can surrender ourselves to the one true God. All it takes is forming a personal relationship with God, through His Son, Jesus Christ, and to study the Scriptures that were given to us to live by. The following two verses address anxiety, fear, and worry.

PHILIPPIANS 4:6-7 – *Do not be anxious about anything, but in every situation, by prayer and petition, with thanksgiving, present your request to God. And the peace of God, which transcends all understanding, will guard your hearts and your minds in Christ Jesus.*

MATTHEW 6:27 – *Can anyone of you by worrying add a single hour to your life?*

October 1 ______________________________

Verse of the Day

MARK 7:20-23

He went on: "What comes out of a person is what defiles them. For it is from within, out of a person's heart, that evil thoughts come—sexual immorality, theft, murder, adultery, greed, malice, deceit, lewdness, envy, slander, arrogance, and folly. All these evils come from inside and defile a person."

If we are not living a godly life, a life based on the teachings of Jesus, it is because we choose to live in sin. Jesus opened the door for all of us. He offers us God's protection, but as I have said before, we also have free will, so it is up to us to seek His help. If life begins to sour, if we fall into one of the categories in this passage, only we can do something about it!

October 2 ______________________________

Verse of the Day

MARK 24:46-48

He told them, "This is what is written: The Messiah will suffer and rise from the dead on the third day, and repentance for the forgiveness of sins will be preached in his name to all nations, beginning at Jerusalem. You are witnesses of these things.

As I mentioned before, what has been prophesied has happened and was witnessed by many. Once we believe in the resurrection because of the facts that prove it, how can we still not study and follow all that Jesus taught? Have you ever wondered how the message that Jesus preached has endured throughout history? How someone that only preached for three years was able to have the most significant impact in all of history? How the Bible is still the most read and printed book ever written? In America alone more than 12 million copies are sold each year, and around the world, the growth is staggering. Can we possibly think this is all by chance? That all those that have tried to disprove the Scriptures have failed to produce any solid evidence to support their claims? Look at how countless numbers of unbelievers converted after trying to prove to others not to believe!

October 3 ______________________________

Verse of the Day

PROVERBS 15:7

The lips of the wise spread knowledge, but the hearts of fools are not upright.

We do not want to follow someone else's agenda or to allow ourselves to be manipulated. Rather we want to follow facts through knowledge.

October 4________________________________

Verse of the Day

PSALM 28:6-7

Praise be to the Lord, for he has heard my cry for mercy. The Lord is my strength and my shield; my heart trusts in him, and he helps me. My heart leaps for joy, and with my song I praise Him.

You have free will. Therefore you can choose to navigate this world alone, or you can accept the most amazing offer ever. I know there is a lot of repetitiveness throughout these verses; it makes me wonder if it was done purposely. God so badly wants us to seek Him before all else, so He can lead us to the promise land, that His message was consistent throughout the Scriptures.

October 5________________________________

Verse of the Day

HEBREWS 12:14-15

Make every effort to live in peace with everyone and to be holy; without holiness no one will see the Lord. See to it that no one falls short of the grace of God and that no bitter root grows up to cause trouble and defile many.

Let us live united, not divided! Surrender to the Lord. If we simply follow the Scriptures and live according to them, we will have what we need—both in this world and the next. Do not be one that divides people or is responsible for leading others down the wrong path, but instead be one that accepts all and unites people.

October 6 ____________________

Verse of the Day

PROVERBS 4:23-27

Above all else, guard your heart, for everything you do flows from it. Keep your mouth free of perversity; keep corrupt talk far from your lips. Let your eyes look straight ahead; fix your gaze directly before you. Give careful thought to the paths for your feet and be steadfast in all your ways. Do not turn to the right or the left; keep your foot from evil.

October 7 ____________________

Verse of the Day

REVELATION 3:10

Since you have kept my command to endure patiently, I will also keep you from the hour of trial that is going to come on the whole world to test the inhabitants of the earth.

There are many passages in the Bible about the end times; those days to come will be like nothing we can imagine. The many people who still discount the warnings in Scripture will be enduring the final trials of this world without the armor of God. Meanwhile the faithful will be lifted away from the trials that are promised to occur. God gave us free will! It is our choice to accept the full protection of our Father or to endure the suffering. I choose to listen to our Fathers warnings!

October 8 ____________________

Verse of the Day

MATTHEW 10:38-39 NLT

If you refuse to take up your cross and follow me, you are not worthy of being mine. If you cling to your life, you will lose it; but if you give up your life for me, you will find it.

God has let us know what He expects from us. Now we need to get our priorities in order. I thank God for opening my eyes.

October 10 ____________________

Verse of the Day

PROVERBS 12:22

The Lord detests lying lips, but he delights in people who are trustworthy.

October 11 ______________________

Verse of the Day

MATTHEW 5:11-12

Blessed are you when people insult you, persecute you, and falsely say all kinds of evil against you because of me. Rejoice and be glad, because great is your reward in heaven, for in the same way they persecuted the prophets who were before you.

We can never let anyone discourage us from our faith. If others are noticing our love of Jesus then we are on the right track. People have recognized my love of Jesus and I wore it as a badge of honor.

I was told from someone very close to me, that some people from my past were trying to insult me. They started calling me Johnny Osteen thinking that this would be something that would embarrass me or hurt me. When I heard about this, I was so happy that my faith was that recognizable. I asked the person that told me this to thank them!

October 12 ______________________

Verse of the Day

1 PETER 1:6-7

In all this you greatly rejoice, though now for a little while you may have had to suffer grief in all kinds of trials. These have come so that the proven genuineness of your faith—of greater worth than gold, which perishes even though refined by fire—may result in praise, glory, and honor when Jesus Christ is revealed.

Once we ask we will receive, but it is earned. God will first release us from bondage, and then we need to walk through the wilderness. Then and only then will He deliver us to the Promised Land, true freedom.

October 13 ______________________________

Verse of the Day

2 PETER 1:2

Grace and peace be yours in abundance through the knowledge of God and of Jesus our Lord.

Merely the knowledge of God and Jesus is far more valuable than any other studies here on Earth. We should take the time to educate ourselves and our families in the Word. Doing so will be the best time spent and best gift we can give to our families.

I love this saying: "Helping one person might not change the whole world, but it could change the world for that one person."

If we wonder how our small contribution can help change anything in the grand scheme of things, the above quote can remind us.

October 14 ________________________________

Verse of the Day

ROMANS 12:17-21

Do not repay anyone evil for evil. Be careful to do what is right in the eyes of everyone. If it is possible, as far as it depends on you, live in peace with everyone. Do not take revenge, my dear friend, but leave room for God's wrath for it is written: "It is mine to avenge; I will repay, says the Lord." On the contrary: "If your enemy is hungry, feed him: if he is thirsty, give him something to drink. In doing this, you will heap burning coals on his head." Do not be overcome by evil, but overcome evil with good.

Forgiveness is not only much more powerful than vengeance, but also much more rewarding. If we let hate control us, we are actually letting *evil* control us. We need to pray for our enemy instead of allowing hate to fester inside of us. It took me most of my life to fully understand this.

October 16 ______________________________

Verse of the Day

ROMANS 8:5-6

Those who live according to the flesh have their minds set on what the flesh desires; but those who live in accordance with the Spirit have their minds set on what the Spirit desires. The mind governed by flesh is death, but the mind governed by the Spirit is life and peace.

It is always our choice, death or life and peace! God gives us the choice to follow Him through His Son Jesus Christ or follow the ways of this world.

October 17 ______________________________

Verse of the Day

EPHESIANS 4:25-27

Therefore each of you must put off falsehood and speak truthfully to your neighbor, for we are all members of one body. In your anger, do not sin. Do not let the sun go down while you are still angry, and do not give the devil a foothold.

We cannot let this world separate us from God. The devil works to divide us and spread hate. If we pray for those that anger us, we will also be freed from evil.

October 18 ________________________________

Verse of the Day

LUKE 12:31-32

But seek his kingdom, and these things will be given to you as well. Do not be afraid, little flock, for your Father has been pleased to give you the kingdom.

So many times throughout Scripture, God offers us the way out—the path of life. Jesus came down to Earth to let us know the plan God has for us and tried to tell us. He is patient, as evidenced by the passing of over 2000 years. God wants us to enter the kingdom through the narrow gate. However, the day will come, like a thief in the night, and then what we chose through our free will be judged.

October 19 ________________________________

Verse of the Day

1 JOHN 2:9-11

Anyone who claims to be in the light but hates a brother or sister is still in the darkness. Anyone who loves their brother and sister lives in the light, and there is nothing in them to make them stumble. But anyone who hates a brother or sister is in the darkness and walks around in the darkness. They do not know where they are going, because the darkness has blinded them.

It is easy to get caught up in saying we hate someone in our life that has wronged us, or to get blinded by hate about things going on in the media. We will always lose when we lead by hate.

October 20 ______________________________

Verse of the Day

PROVERBS 15:8

A hot tempered person stirs up conflict. But the one who is patient calms a quarrel.

October 21 ______________________________

Verse of the Day

EPHESIANS 6:18

And pray in the Spirit on all occasions with all kinds of prayers and requests. With this in mind, be alert and always keep on praying for all the Lord's people.

Our pastor said yesterday, "Preparation is the key to victory." This saying is in many sports teams' locker rooms. Can you imagine what could happen if we put the same emphasis on preparation for the promise of eternal life as these teams do before a game?

October 22

Verse of the Day

MATTHEW 21:28:32

The Parable of the Two Sons
(Jesus speaking to the Pharisees and others.)

"What do you think? There was a man who had two sons. He went to the first and said, 'Son, go and work today in the vineyard.' 'I will not,' he answered, but later he changed his mind and went.

"Then the father went to the other son and said the same thing. He answered, 'I will sir,' but he did not go. Which of the two did what the father wanted?" "The first," they answered.

Jesus said to them, "Truly, I tell you, the tax collectors and the prostitutes are entering the kingdom of God ahead of you. For John came to show you the way of righteousness, and you did not believe him, but the tax collectors and the prostitutes did. And even after you saw this, you did not repent and believe him."

Which son are you? I've been told by the Father many times to follow. I didn't act right away, but now I do. Anyone can be saved, we just have to believe and do what the Father is asking of us. The elitist Pharisees thought they knew better. They were more concerned about their worldly beliefs, rituals, and power than obeying God.

October 23 ________________________________

Verse of the Day

MATTHEW 22:36-37

"Teacher, which is the greatest commandment in the Law?" Jesus replied: "Love the Lord your God with all your heart and with all your soul and with all your mind."

October 24 ________________________________

Verse of the Day

PROVERBS 21:2

A person may think their own ways are right, but the Lord weighs the heart.

October 25 ________________________________

Verse of the Day

MATTHEW 26:3-4

Then the chief priest and the elders of the people assembled in the palace of the high priest, whose name was Caiaphas, and they schemed to arrest Jesus secretly and kill him.

Jesus threatened the power of the corrupt establishment of His time. Through lies and schemes, they deceived and convinced the people to put Jesus to death over Barabbas, a murderer, even after witnessing all the good Jesus had done. We must be careful not to be deceived by those in power like the masses who followed blindly and put Jesus to death. So many will believe things that are told to them without questioning motives. The ones in power manipulate others mainly through hate, fear, and lies—be aware of these things.

October 26 ______________________________

Verse of the Day

REVELATION 21:6-8

He said to me: "It is done. I am the Alpha and the Omega, the Beginning and the End. To the thirsty, I will give water without cost from the springs of life. Those who are victorious will inherit all this, and I will be their God and they will be my children. But the cowardly, the unbelieving, the vile, the murderers, the sexually immoral, those who practice magic arts, the idolaters, and all the liars—they will be consigned to the fiery lake of burning sulfur. This is the second death."

We are all God's children; He gives us a choice to turn from evil ways and avoid what is to come.

October 27 ________________________

Verse of the Day

PROVERBS 2:6-8

For the Lord gives wisdom; from his mouth come knowledge and understanding. He holds success in store for the upright, he is a shield to those whose walk is blameless, for he guards the course of the just and protects the way of his faithful ones.

October 29 ________________________

Verse of the Day

ISAIAH 5:20

Woe to those who call evil good and good evil, who put darkness for light and light for darkness, who put bitter for sweet and sweet for bitter.

We need to be careful about what we believe and whom we follow. This verse evokes our present-day life. It is not possible to have sound judgment with a hateful mind.

October 31 ________________________________

Verse of the Day

JOHN 17:1-3

After Jesus said this, he looked toward the heaven and prayed, "Father, the hour has come. Glorify your Son, that your Son may glorify you. For you granted him authority over all people that he might give eternal life to all those you have given him. Now this is eternal life: that they know you, the only true God, and Jesus Christ, whom you have sent.

Are we ready to accept the most amazing gift of all, or will we just keep making excuses and criticizing without researching Scriptures? Will we continue to try to live life our way? Do we fully grasp that if we are wrong, the biggest price paid will be by ourselves and our children?

CHAPTER 12

November

I wanted to share another set of verses that have had a profound effect on me and have been a big part of my spiritual journey. I have had to fight addictions, doubt, envy, lust, and a list of other evil traps.

A friend of mine, Ron, gave me a coin with the armor of God on it, which he received from his men's group. The coin shows all the parts of God's armor along with the words of Ephesians 6:11-18, "Put on the full armor of God. Pray always." I now carry a coin with me and try to pass them out to help others as it helped me.

This set of verses will help us to fight against the ever-so-real spiritual battle that is waged for our souls. Evil is constantly working to turn us towards the dark side. It may start with little things that do not seem like sins. But left unprotected, evil will consume us, whether we are dealing with issues like drug addiction, alcohol addiction, pornography, lust, infidelity, deceit, doubt, hate, or the many other temptations leading only to ruin. God offers us His help, His protection, but He also gives us free will to make the choice to accept his offer or to refuse it.

November 1 ______________________

Verse of the Day

EPHESIANS 6:10-20

Finally, be strong in the Lord and his mighty power. Put on the full armor of God, so that you can take a stand against the devil's schemes. For our struggle is not against flesh and blood, but against the powers of this dark world and against the spiritual forces of evil in the heavenly realms. Therefore put on the full armor of God, so that when the day of evil comes, you may be able to stand your ground, and after you have done everything, to stand.

Stand firm then, with the belt of truth buckled around your waist, with the breastplate of righteousness in place, and with your feet fitted with the readiness that comes from the gospel of peace. In addition to all this, take up the shield of faith, with which you can extinguish all the flaming arrows of the evil one.

Take the helmet of salvation and the sword of the Spirit, which is the word of God. And then pray in the Spirit on all occasions with all kinds of prayers and requests. With this in mind, be alert and always keep on praying for all the Lords people. Pray also for me, that whenever I speak, words may be given me so that I will fearlessly make known the mystery of the gospel, for which I am an ambassador in chains. Pray that I may declare it fearlessly, as I should.

Ten Verses about Prayer

PHILIPPIANS 4:6 – *"Do not be anxious about anything, but in everything, by prayer and petition, with thanksgiving, present your requests to God."*

JAMES 5:16 – *"Therefore confess your sins to each other and pray for each other so that you may be healed. The prayer of a righteous man is powerful and effective."*

1 JOHN 1:9 – *"If we confess our sins, he is faithful and just and will forgive us our sins and purify us from all unrighteousness.*

JEREMIAH 29:12 – *"Then you will call on me and come and pray to me, and I will listen to you."*

JEREMIAH 33:3 – *"Call to me and I will answer you and tell you great and unsearchable things you do not know."*

LUKE 6:27-28 – *"But to you who are listening I say: Love your enemies, do good to those who hate you, bless those who curse you, pray for those who mistreat you."*

MATTHEW 6:6 – *"But when you pray, go into your room, close the door and pray to your Father, who is unseen. Then your Father, who sees what is done in secret, will reward you."*

PSALM 18:6 – *"In my distress I called to the Lord; I cried to my God for help. From his temple he heard my voice; my cry came before him, into his ears."*

MARK 11:24 – *"Therefore I tell you, whatever you ask for in prayer, believe that you have received it, and it will be yours."*

1 THESSALONIANS 5:16-18 – *"Rejoice always, pray without ceasing, give thanks in all circumstances; for this is the will of God in Christ Jesus for you."*

November 2____________________________

Verse of the Day

PROVERBS 19:20

Listen to advice and accept discipline, and at the end you will be counted among the wise.

November 4____________________________

Verse of the Day

PROVERBS 3:1-2

My son, do not forget my teaching, but keep my commands in your heart, for they will prolong your life many years and bring you peace and prosperity.

November 5

Verse of the Day

1 TIMOTHY 4:7-8

Have nothing to do with godless myths and old wives tales; rather, train yourself to be godly. For physical training is of some value, but godliness has value for all things, holding promise for both the present life and the life to come.

We train for all kinds of things—sports, music, careers, military—we are not just automatically great at these things. We need to put that same effort into our spiritual training, it takes commitment, hard work, and dedication to stay on a godly path.

November 8

Verse of the Day

ACTS 7:51-53

You stiff-necked people! Your hearts and your ears are still uncircumcised. You are just like your ancestors: You always resist the Holy Spirit! Was there ever a prophet your ancestors did not persecute? They even killed those who predicted the coming of the Righteous One. And now you have betrayed and murdered him, you who have received the law that was given through angels but have not obeyed it.

It is sad that people allow themselves to be misled. God is patient, God is kind, but He is also just! I don't know how many warnings people need!

November 11 ______________________________

Verse of the Day

2 CHRONICLES 20:12

Our God, will you not judge them? For they have no power to face this vast army that is attacking us. We do not know what to do, but our eyes are on you.

Keep your eyes on God; He is always there for us. So many just choose not to stay in faith and then drift further and further away from God. An enemy is always on the attack, looking for entry into our lives, but God is always there for us if we just trust and stay in relationship with Him.

November 13 ______________________________

Verse of the Day

DEUTERONOMY 31:6

Be strong and courageous. Do not be afraid or terrified because of them, for the Lord your God goes with you; he will never leave you nor forsake you.

God is and has always been there for us. It is our choice to seek His help and guidance or to ignore it and walk through this world unprotected. "Seek and you will find," and then we will know what it feels like to be content.

November 14 ______________________

Verse of the Day

ROMANS 10:9

If you declare with your mouth, "Jesus is Lord," and believe in your heart that God raised him from the dead, you will be saved.

No comment needed.

November 15 ______________________

Verse of the Day

1 JOHN 4:7-8

Dear friends, let us love one another, for love comes from God. Everyone who loves has been born of God and knows God. Whoever does not love does not know God, because God is Love.

If we allow ourselves to be guided by hate of a neighbor, a co-worker, an ex-spouse, or a politician, then we are allowing the devil a foothold into our lives. When I pray instead for those who have wronged me, or whom I disagree with, I invite God into my life, not evil.

Additional Verse

ROMANS 14:11-12

It is written: "As surely as I live, says the Lord, every knee will bow before me; every tongue will acknowledge God." So then, each of us will give an account of ourselves to God.

If tomorrow were the day to give account, would we be prepared? If I am wrong in my beliefs, then I simply will have lived a life that was kind, peaceful, and content—a life of trying to spread love and peace. Who can be sure that we do not need to live a God-filled life, according to the Scriptures? Who is so sure that they would risk God's promise to us?

November 16 ______________________________

Verse of the Day

1 CORINTHIANS 1:18-19

For the message of the cross is foolishness to those who are perishing, but to us who are being saved it is the power of God. For it is written: I will destroy the wisdom of the wise; the intelligence of the intelligent I will frustrate.

Some think they are educated and intelligent by worldly standards, but they are blind and lacking the wisdom God offers. God has taken that ability from them because of their ways.

November 19 ______________________________

Verse of the Day

2 PETER 3:9

The Lord is not slow to keep his promise, as some understand slowness. Instead he is patient with you, not wanting anyone to perish, but everyone to come to repentance.

God wants us to have salvation; He has given mankind many opportunities to be with Him for eternity. However, the time will come when that opportunity is no longer offered, and I just hope we are all prepared.

November 20 ______________________________

Verse of the Day

PROVERBS 19:16

Whoever keeps commandments keeps their life, but whoever shows contempt for their ways will die.

Do people understand that Jesus is offering us eternal life? He is also warning us of what will happen if we show contempt for His teachings.

November 21 ______________________

Verse of the Day

JAMES 1:19-22

My dear brothers and sisters, take note of this: Everyone should be quick to listen, slow to speak and slow to anger, because human anger does not produce the righteousness that God desires. Therefore, get rid of all moral filth and the evil that is so prevalent and humbly accept the word planted in you, which can save you. Do not merely listen to the word, and so deceive yourself. Do what it says.

God offered us everlasting life—eternity with Him in peace. We can hear the offer, but more importantly, we have to act on it.

November 22 ______________________

Verse of the Day

2 CORINTHIANS 9:6-7

Remember this: Whoever sows sparingly will also reap sparingly, and whoever sows generously will reap generously. Each of you should give what you have decided in your heart to give, not reluctantly or under compulsion, for God loves a cheerful giver.

We have all heard the saying, "You reap what you sow." Once we can give joyfully of our time and our money, then we will please God. Once we also understand that all is God's in the first place and we are only stewards of what He gives us, we will see that giving the first of what we have is an act of faith. God will then reward us accordingly. God does not need money; He wants only to see how strong our faith is.

Additional Verse

PROVERBS 12:19

Truthful lips endure forever, but a lying tongue lasts only a moment.

We live in a world and time of many lies. History will expose those who lie for their own power and greed, just as it always has. Those who are deceitful will pass and the truth will endure.

November 23 ________________________________

Verse of the Day

JOHN 7:37-39

On the last and greatest day of the festival, Jesus stood and said in a loud voice, "Let anyone who is thirsty come to me and drink. Whoever believes in me, as the Scriptures have said, rivers of living water will flow from within them." By this he meant the Spirit, whom those who believe in him were later to receive. Up to that time the Spirit has not been given, since Jesus had not yet been glorified.

It is like the saying, "It's a catch 22." We will not know how great the Spirit of God is—or receive it—until we believe, but we doubt because we have never experienced what Jesus offered us, which is the Holy Spirit. We first have to surrender ourselves until we can understand. That is faith!

November 24 ______________________________

Verse of the Day

PSALM 128:1-2

Blessed are all who fear the Lord, who walk in obedience to him. You will eat the fruit of your labor; blessing and prosperity will be yours.

I cannot think of a better investment. I invest my obedience to the Word, to God, and the Lord Jesus, and in return the dividends are His blessings, prosperity, and oh yeah—eternal life! God is love! We all sin, but to be obedient we must confess those sins and ask for God's forgiveness.

November 25 ______________________________

Verse of the Day

LUKE 8:16-18

No one lights a lamp and hides it in a clay jar or puts it under a bed. Instead, they put it on a stand, so that those who come can see the light. For there is nothing hidden that will not be disclosed, and nothing concealed that will not be known or brought out into the open. Therefore consider carefully how you listen. Whoever has will be given more; whoever does not have, even what they think they have will be taken from them.

When we do wrong we begin to distance ourselves from God—we hide. However, if we recognize our sins and ask God for forgiveness, He will always be there for us. In turn, when we are walking on the narrow path with God, our light shines for everyone to see.

November 26 ______________________________

Verse of the Day

JAMES 3:14-16

But if you harbor bitter envy and selfish ambition in your hearts, do not boast about it or deny the truth. Such "wisdom" does not come down from heaven but is earthly, unspiritual, demonic. For where you have envy and selfish ambition, there you find disorder and every evil practice.

Do not allow the devil to enter your body through jealousy or any other self-inflicted method; this is just another way for evil to take a grip on you and your life. If you know the scriptures and live them in your everyday life, you will then have what you need to stay protected.

November 27 ______________________________

Verse of the Day

PROVERBS 3:5-6

Trust in the Lord with all your heart and lean not on your own understanding; in all your ways submit to him, and he will make your paths straight.

These words describe what faith means to me. Doubt, anxiety, and discouragement come from evil! When I trust in the Lord, these things start to fade away.

Additional Verse

PSALM 32:9-10

Do not be like the horse or the mule, which have no understanding but must be controlled by bit and bridle or they will not come to you. Many are the woes of the wicked, but the Lord's unfailing love surrounds the one who trusts in him.

Trust in the Lord. Do not be controlled by this world. I found that once I took the time to learn the Scriptures, I began to have a much clearer understanding of the world around me. I still have a long way to go, I look forward to learning more every day.

November 28 – Thanksgiving ______________________

Verse of the Day

1 THESSALONIANS 5:16

"Rejoice always, pray continually, give thanks in all circumstances; for this is God's will for you in Christ Jesus."

I want to be thankful everyday not just today, and let God know that I am.

November 29 ______________________________

Verse of the Day

PROVERBS 14:30

A heart of peace gives life to the body, but envy rots the bones.

Sometimes no comment is necessary!

November 30 ______________________________

Verse of the Day

MATTHEW 28:16-20

Then the eleven disciples went to Galilee, to the mountain where Jesus had told them to go. When they saw him, they worshiped him; but some doubted. Then Jesus came to them and said, "All authority in heaven and on earth has been given to me. Therefore, go and make disciples of all nations, baptizing them in the name of the Father and the Son and the Holy Spirit, and teaching them to obey everything I have commanded you. And surely I am with you always, to the very end of the age."

The coming of Jesus and the Resurrection are the most important events to have ever happened in human history. Many have tried to disprove these events. Many people who were unable to do so became believers and began to worship.

CHAPTER 13

December

December 1

Verse of the Day

GALATIANS 6:7-8

Do not be deceived: God cannot be mocked. A man reaps what he sows. Whoever sows to please their flesh, from the flesh will reap destruction; whoever sows to please the Spirit from the Spirit will reap eternal life.

December 2

Verse of the Day

ACTS 4:12

Salvation is found in no one else, for there is no other name under heaven given to mankind by which we must be saved.

So many resist the teachings of Jesus and want to create their own beliefs, or live according to this Earth instead of accepting the Holy Spirit. I know much of what my thoughts reflect seems repetitive. However, throughout the Bible, the message was repeated: God wants us to have salvation!

December 3 ______________________

Verse of the Day

PROVERBS 11:4

Wealth is worthless in the day of wrath, but righteousness delivers from death.

Are we storing up our earthly dollars on things, or are we investing in our spiritual future? I picture this cartoon of a hearse towing a U-Haul truck! You can't take it with you, it's all worthless! However, if you invested your time in scripture and knowing God, the reward would be priceless!

December 4 ______________________

Verse of the Day

LUKE 24:44-48

He said to them, "This is what I told you while I was still with you: Everything must be fulfilled that was written about me in the Law of Moses, the Prophets, and the Psalms." Then he opened their minds so they could understand the Scriptures. He told them, "This is what is written: The Messiah will suffer and rise from the dead on the third day, and repentance for the forgiveness of sins will be preached in his name to all nations, beginning with Jerusalem. You are witnesses of these things."

This is so important. Jesus fulfilled the Scriptures and prophecies written long before His birth. Jesus appeared after His Resurrection to 500 people at one time. This was well-documented, scribes were a daily part of living in those days. Jesus performed many miracles that thousands of people witnessed. After His death, His words have spread to all corners of the earth reaching and affecting billions of people. Yet in spite of witnesses to His many miracles, people still doubt Him. The price we pay for this doubt is the ultimate price.

We are what we feed our minds. Try to start your day in daily prayer, just take 5 minutes each morning to start a routine of praying. Take a 30-day challenge, you have much more to gain than you have to lose.

December 5 ______________________________

Verse of the Day

EPHESIANS 4:29-32

Do not let any unwholesome talk come out of your mouths, but only what is helpful for building others up according to their needs, that it may benefit those who listen. And do not grieve the Holy Spirit of God, with whom you were sealed for the day of redemption. Get rid of all bitterness, rage and anger, brawling and slander, along with every form of malice. Be kind and compassionate to one another, forgive each other, just as in Christ God forgave you.

How can anyone speak badly of these teachings? Probably because they don't take the time to read them or understand them. The only path to learning the Word is through surrender, so we then walk with the Holy Spirit. Jesus forgave us our sins, washed them clean, so how can we think it is right not to forgive those who sin against us or hurt us?

December 7 ________________________________

Verse of the Day

MATTHEW 5:6

Blessed are those who hunger and thirst for righteousness, for they will be filled.

We must put in the effort to receive the reward. We must want a relationship with God.

December 8 ______________________________

Verse of the Day

2 THESSALONIANS 2:10-12

And all the ways that wickedness deceives those who are perishing. They perish because they refuse to love the truth and so be saved. For this reason, God sends them a powerful delusion so that they will believe the lie and so that all will be condemned who have not believed the truth but have delighted in wickedness.

Those who live godless lives will be blinded from the truth, and believe in the delusions. Only through the guidance of the Holy Spirit and the surrendering to God's will the truth be known—and the truth will set us free!

December 9 ______________________________

Verse of the Day

PHILIPPIANS 2:14-16

Do everything without grumbling or arguing, so that you may become blameless and pure, "children of God without fault in a warped and crooked generation." Then you will shine among them like stars in the sky as you hold firmly to the word of life. And then I will be able to boast on the day of Christ that I did not run or labor in vain.

Hold firmly to the word of life! Don't go through life complaining and at odds with others. God is offering us everlasting life in Him. Is there anything else more important in which we can invest our time and effort?

December 10 ______________________

Verse of the Day

2 CORINTHIANS 5:17-20 NLT

This means that anyone who belongs to Christ has become a new person. The old is gone; a new life has begun! And all of this is a gift from God, who brought us back to himself through Christ. And God has given us this task of reconciling people to him. For God was in Christ, reconciling the world to himself, no longer counting people's sins against them. And he gave us this wonderful message of reconciliations. So we are Christ's ambassadors; God makes his appeal through us. We speak for Christ when we plead, "Come back to God!"

December 11 ______________________

Verse of the Day

MATTHEW 7:13-14

Enter through the narrow gate. For wide is the gate and broad is the road that leads to destruction, and many enter through it. But small is the gate and narrow the road that leads to life, and only a few find it.

Why mess with the afterlife? Jesus gave us the road map. It takes dedication to follow it, but look at the alternative vs. the reward. We train diligently and study for jobs, sports, and fitness, but so many spend no time training for what God, Jesus, and the prophets told and promised us. Look around: many are heading towards the wide gate. My efforts are geared toward entering through that narrow gate.

December 12

Verse of the Day

ROMANS 8:9-10 NLT

But you are not controlled by your sinful nature. You are controlled by the Spirit of God living in you. (And remember that those who do not have the Spirit of Christ living in them do not belong to him at all.) And Christ lives within you, so even though your body will die because of sin, the Spirit gives you life because you have been made right with God.

Trying to explain to a non-believer what the Spirit of God feels like in me is difficult because it is something that must be experienced. Those full of doubt and not committed, as I was for most of my life, cannot grasp the true experience. All

I can say is that once you do surrender and commit yourself, the results are amazing—not easy, but amazing!

December 13________________________________

Verse of the Day

PROVERBS 19:1

Better the poor whose walk is blameless then a fool whose lips are perverse.

December 14________________________________

Verse of the Day

JOHN 3:20:21 NLT

All who do evil hate the light and refuse to go near it for fear their sins will be exposed. But those who do what is right come to the light so others can see that they are doing what God wants.

God is the light. Righteousness and following Jesus is the light. When we are doing wrong and covering up shame, we avoid the very things that will save us. If we only would realize that when God is in our life, He can pull us out of the darkness and set us free.

December 15

Verse of the Day

JOHN 12:31

Now is the time for judgement on this world; now the prince of this world will be driven out. And I, when lifted up from the earth, will draw all people to myself.

Jesus spent only three years preaching, fulfilling many of the prophecies written hundreds and even thousands of years before His birth. From His death and resurrection to date, billions of people have followed him. In the history of the world no other person has had such an impact. Yet so many still doubt or do not take the time to try to understand. We need to ask ourselves if any of this sounds important enough to take the time to do the research. Many scholars and some of the brightest minds in history have concluded the evidence is overwhelming on issues like the Resurrection, Jesus's birth, His time on Earth, and the prophesies.

If the facts and the evidence supports the claims of Christianity, then verses like the one above and all the others are monumental. When judgment is ready for this world, I just pray you are ready.

December 16

Verse of the Day

1 JOHN 2:9-11

Anyone who claims to be in the light but hates a brother or sister is still in the darkness. Anyone who loves their brother and sister lives in the light, and there is nothing to make them stumble. But anyone who hates a brother or sister is in the darkness and walks around in the darkness. They do not know where they are going, because the darkness has blinded them.

The devil will use hate to mislead us and we will not be able to see truth. Brothers and sisters account for everyone on Earth, if we hate our neighbor, coworker, a politician, or any other, we have let evil in, and will be blind to understanding truth. If we pray for that group or person, we will be protected from the evil trying to creep into our life.

Not too long ago, I realized I was full of hate for a group of people and it was consuming me. One night at a church small group meeting, I spoke up about how I harbored hate for Radical Islam. I served in the Iran-Iraq war in the Persian Gulf. I realized I had held onto this hate for so long, but that night God freed me from it. I announced to the group that from then on, I would pray for my enemies. I still believe that they are led by evil, and I completely condemn their actions. I now know that they need all of our prayers in order to find

Jesus, so they too can be set free. By doing this, I was set free. It is an amazing feeling. Thank you God!

December 17 ______________________

Verse of the Day

JOHN 18:36 NLT

Jesus answered, "My Kingdom is not of this earthly kingdom. If it were, my followers would fight to keep me from being handed over to the Jewish leaders. But my Kingdom is not from this world."

We can continue to hold onto the things and ways of this world or prepare for what is next. Jesus threatened the powerful of that time; He knew their hearts were not right.

December 18 ______________________

Verse of the Day

2 PETER 3:9

The Lord is not slow in keeping his promise, as some understand slowness. Instead he is patient with you, not wanting anyone to perish, but everyone to come to repentance.

We are being given our chance for salvation, but the day will come, like a thief in the night, and we will have either prepared ourselves through what Jesus teaches us, or we will perish.

December 19

Verse of the Day

2 CHRONICLES 7:14

If my people, who are called by my name, will humble themselves and pray and seek my face and turn from their wicked ways, then I will hear from heaven, and I will forgive their sins and will heal their land.

We can do it our way, but it is always better to do it God's way. Have you heard the saying, "Nothing is free?" God is asking for our commitment to get all that He offers—it's our choice! We get back what we put in and we reap what we sow!

December 20

Verse of the Day

PROVERBS 29:2

When the righteous thrive, the people rejoice; when the wicked rule, the people groan.

We have some very corrupt leaders tearing apart our world. Take away their rule; do not allow corrupt people to be leaders. Most importantly, don't allow hate to cloud your judgement; rely on facts that are not distorted by those seeking power. I pray for our faithful leaders that they may wear the full armor of God to protect them.

December 21 ______________________________

Verse of the Day

PROVERBS 28:13

Whoever conceals their sins does not prosper, but the one who confesses and renounces them finds mercy.

God knows we are all sinners; all He asks of us is to own up to our mistakes and ask for His forgiveness. The word "prosper" is not only a financial term; we may still do okay financially as our sins eat us up mentally, spiritually, and physically. God is there for us. Confessing to Him directly will set us free. Whenever we sin and do not repent, we move further and further away from God.

December 22 ______________________________

Verse of the Day

MATTHEW 16:26

What good will it be for someone to gain the whole world. Yet forfeit their soul? For the Son of Man is going to come in his Father's glory with angles, and then he will reward each person according to what they have done.

When we die, which of the two will be more important—the things we accumulated while on Earth or what we did to prepare for the judgment of God? We need to spend our time wisely! Use your time to invest in spiritual training. It will pay huge dividends.

Quote of the Day: "If you get your guidance from the wrong place, you will for sure end up on the wrong path."

December 23

Verse of the Day

JOHN 14:8-10

Philip said, "Lord, show us the Father and that will be enough for us."

Jesus answered: "Don't you know me, Philip, even after I have been among you such a long time? Anyone who has seen me has seen the Father. How can you say, 'Show us the Father'? Don't you believe that I am in the Father and the Father is in me? The words I say to you I don't speak on my own authority. Rather, it is the Father, living in me, who is doing his work."

This verse shows the magnitude of the importance of knowing the teachings of Jesus. He is telling us that all of His words are God's words. As I said before, growing up I was not raised in a religious family. We believed in God and Jesus, but did not speak much about our faith. My grandmother was the only person in my life—until my 50s—that instilled in me the Word of God and the importance of knowing Jesus. Even with her influence, I never really understood what is so clear and simple to me now.

It was only about two years ago that I finally understood what it meant when people say "In the name of the Father, the Son, and the Holy Spirit" while making the Sign of the Cross. Once I understood that Jesus was God on Earth and that Jesus left us with the gift of the Holy Spirit, I knew I needed to invest more of my time and life into learning as much as God would show me.

No matter what gets us started on our journey, the important thing is that we *do* get started. It was a few years ago that a Navy shipmate whom I hadn't seen for more than thirty years, Larry Stealey, came into town. Tina and I met Larry and his wife, Tina, for lunch before they left on a cruise vacation. On that day I began another leg of my journey.

Larry had found God and I could feel how it had affected him. He recommended a movie to Tina and me, *A Case for Christ.* It is based on the true story of a *Chicago Tribune* editor, Lee Strobel, who was an atheist. Lee's wife found God after an incident in a restaurant that nearly left their child dead. His wife and her newfound faith were tearing apart their marriage, so Lee decided to set out—as the investigative reporter he was—to prove that Jesus and His resurrection were nothing but a hoax.

To this day Lee goes around telling his story and is a firm believer in Christ. I won't ruin the story for you, but this suggestion from a longtime friend and shipmate opened my eyes in a way that made me want to learn as much as I possibly could about the true faith that Jesus and the Scriptures are trying to teach us about. Thank you, Larry!

I hope everyone finds what sparks his or her journey. Maybe someone in your life will make a suggestion that will change your life beyond measure.

December 24

Verse of the Day

ROMANS 15:13 NLT

I pray that God, the source of hope, will fill you completely with joy and peace because you trust him. Then you will overflow with confident hope through the power of the Holy Spirit.

In God we trust! The rewards are amazing. Our country knew this years ago, so much so we put it on our money and in the fabric of our society. Let us not forget the virtues our founding fathers espoused. I have learned to have joy and peace always, to not let the trials of this world get me down, because I know I will always have God with me.

I am not sure where I heard the following words, but they have remained with me: "If I know I will have eternal life, what can possibly take that joy away? No matter what happens today or how bad things get, I will always know this." It just doesn't get any better than that!

December 25

Verse of the Day

COLOSSIANS 1:15 NLT

Christ is the visible image of the invisible God. He exsisted before anything was created and is supreme over all creation

Merry Christmas! This is an amazing verse and we need to take time to think about that!

> The greatest man in history, named Jesus, had no servants, yet they called Him Master; had no degree, yet they called Him Teacher; had no medicines, yet they called Him Healer.
> He had no army, yet kings feared Him. He won no military battles, yet He conquered the world.
> He committed no crime, yet they crucified Him.
> He was buried in a tomb, yet He lives today.
>
> (Source unknown.)

December 26 ______________________________

Verse of the Day

GALATIANS 1:4-5 NLT

Jesus gave his life for our sins just as God the Father planned, in order to rescue us from this evil world in which we live. All glory to God forever and ever! Amen.

God has given us a way to live in this world with His help. He also gave us a path to enter His kingdom. Thank you, Father!

December 28 ______________________________

Verse of the Day

LUKE 6:45 NLT

A good person produces good things from the treasury of a good heart, and an evil person produces evil things from the treasury of an evil heart. What you say flows from what is in your heart.

We must guard our words and think before we speak because our words reflect who we are, especially in God's eyes. It is much better to speak good words, knowing that we have lifted someone up, than to allow ourselves to fall into the devil's evil traps.

December 29

Verse of the Day

MATTHEW 6:31-34 NLT

So don't worry about these things, saying, 'What will we eat? What will we drink? What will we wear?' These things dominate the thoughts of unbelievers, but your Heavenly Father already knows what you need. Seek the Kingdom of God above all else, and live righteously, and he will give you everything you need. So don't worry about tomorrow, for tomorrow will bring its own worries. Today's trouble is enough for today.

This describes faith—trusting God fully. With trust also comes contentment. Unbelievers are rarely content because they do not know how to put their full trust in God. Most put their trust in this world instead. I try to live by these words: "I can have everything and still have nothing; I can also have nothing and still have everything." The meaning to me is God is everything! We see so many people who seem to have it all—money, power, and fame—yet they still seem to be unhappy.

December 30

Verse of the Day

PSALM 119:33-37

Teach me, Lord, the way of your decrees, that I may follow it to the end.
Give me understanding, so that I may keep your law and obey it with all my heart.
Direct me in the path of your commands, for there I find delight.
Turn my heart towards your statutes and not towards selfish gain.
Turn my eyes away from worthless things; preserve my life according to your word.

Are we praying for the right things? Once we surrender ourselves to God, we need to develop a personal relationship with Him, and *then* our lives will change. He is always there for us!

December 31

Verse of the Day

1 PETER 1:6-7 NLT

So be truly glad. There is a wonderful joy ahead even though you must endure many trials for a little while. These trials will show that your faith is genuine. It is being tested as fire tests and purifies gold—though your faith is far more precious than mere gold. So when your faith remains strong through many trials, it will bring you much praise and glory and honor on the day when Jesus Christ is revealed to the whole world.

Accepting and surrendering yourself to God does not mean that everything in your life becomes perfect. Rather, it means that we will be tested, and we will be required to do our part. I heard this quote and it stuck with me: "God will first release you from bondage, then you need to walk through the wilderness, and then He will deliver you to the promised land of freedom."

Persevere! Show commitment!

Ten Verses about Love

I cheated on this section and included fourteen verses because of the importance the Scriptures place on Love! I will finish with this.

JOHN 3:16 – *"For God loved the world in this way: He gave his one and only Son, so that everyone who believes in him will not perish but have eternal life."*

ROMANS 8:28 – *We know that all things work together for the good of those who love God, who are called according to his purpose.*

PSALM 23:6 – *Only goodness and faithful love will pursue me all the days of my life, and I will dwell in the house of the Lord as long as I live.*

1 CORINTHIANS 13:4 – *Love is patient, love is kind. Love does not envy, is not boastful, is not arrogant.*

1 CORINTHIANS 13:6 – *Love finds no joy in unrighteousness, but rejoices in the truth.*

GALATIANS 5:22-23 – *But the fruit of the Spirit is love, joy, peace, patience, kindness, goodness, faithfulness, gentleness, and self-control.*

2 TIMOTHY 1:7 – *For God has not given us a spirit of fear, but one of power, love, and sound judgment.*

1 CORINTHIANS 13:8 – *Love never fails. But where there are prophecies, they will cease; where there are tongues, they will be stilled; where there is knowledge, it will pass away.*

ROMANS 5:8 – *But God demonstrates his own love for us in this: While we were still sinners, Christ died for us.*

1 CORINTHIANS 13:13 – *And now these three remain: faith, hope, and love. But the greatest of these is love.*

PSALM 91:14 – *"Because he loves me," says the Lord, "I will rescue him; I will protect him, for he acknowledges my name."*

JOHN 15:13 – *Greater love has no one than this: to lay down one's life for one's friends.*

GALATIANS 2:20 – *I have been crucified with Christ and I no longer live, but Christ lives in me. The life I now live in the body, I live by faith in the Son of God, who loved me and gave himself for me.*

ROMANS 8:39 – *Neither height nor depth, nor anything else in all creation, will be able to separate us from the love of God that is in Christ Jesus our Lord.*

About the Author

John Galanti rose from a background that wasn't easy, like so many others. While he enjoyed the love of his family, John always had this feeling that there was something missing.Once finding God, surrendering himself and making a commitment to a daily spiritual journey, John began to understand what it was to have true contentment in all situations.

John Galanti
PO Box 3691
Tequesta, FL 33469

email: john@theaveragejohn.org
web: www.theaveragejohn.org

More Books

For more books by this author, please search John Galanti on Amazon.com